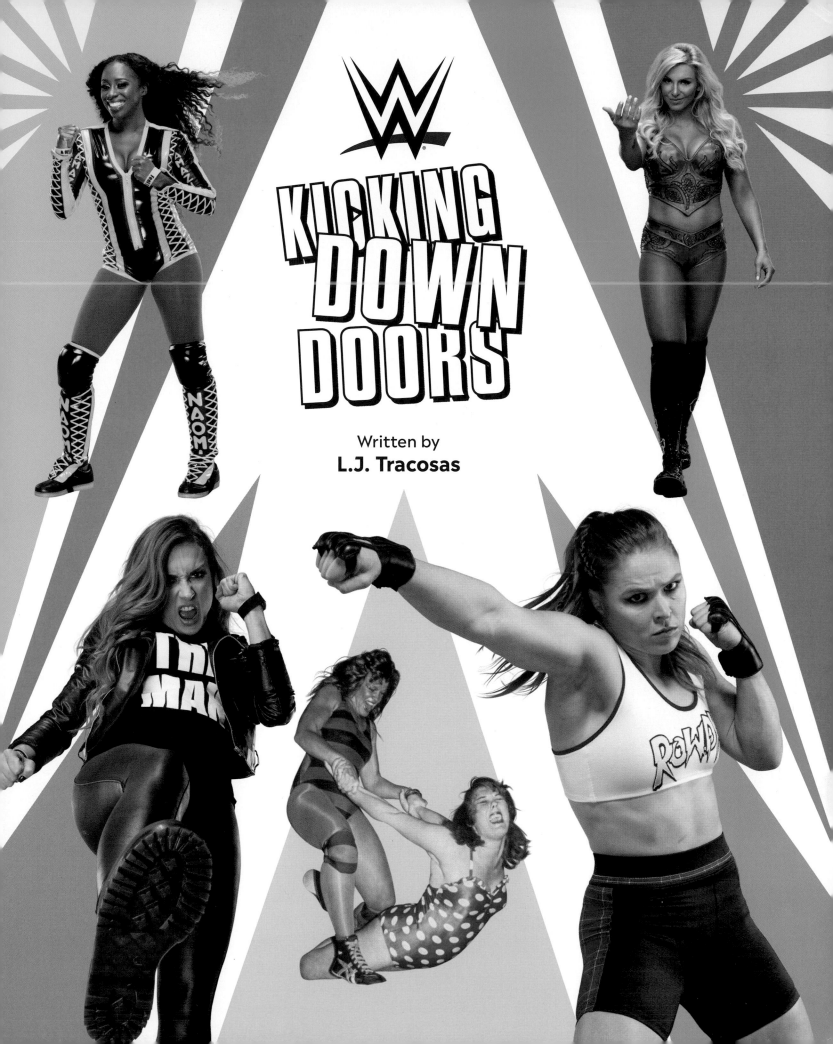

WWE

KICKING DOWN DOORS

Written by
L.J. Tracosas

CONTENTS

Bull Nakano, page 22.

Chyna, page 36.

Sasha Banks, page 90.

THE FIRST FABULOUS FEMALES

Before WWE Superstars and "Divas," there were female competitors such as Josie Wahlford (the first ever Women's World Champion, 1890s), Cora Livingston (World Champion, 1910), and Clara Mortensen (World Champion, 1932). Competing at a time when women were just winning the right to vote, female athletes like these totally reshaped ideas of what women were capable of. They inspired future WWE competitors such as Mildred Burke, Mae Young, and The Fabulous Moolah. And it's lucky they did, because when WWE went national, female competitors had a place at the mat. Women appeared on television with a range of popular and colorful characters such as Hulk Hogan, André the Giant, and the Iron Sheik, during the golden age of sports entertainment.

Mildred Burke displays the Women's World Championship, which she held for two decades.

AHEAD OF THEIR TIME

THE EARLY PIONEERS OF WOMEN IN SPORTS ENTERTAINMENT

Mildred Burke, Mae Young, The Fabulous Moolah, and Judy Grable were champions long before WWE even existed. Competing in the 1930s, Mildred Burke was more than 50 years ahead of her time. With an incredible physique and toughness to match, she battled both female and male athletes.

Mildred was the NWA's Women's Champion for two decades, trained new stars, and toured worldwide, bringing sports entertainment to places such as Japan—the future training ground for 1980s Superstars such as Bull Nakano and Alundra Blayze.

Legend has it that when Mildred traveled to Oklahoma, a young woman named Mae Young showed up to challenge the champ. From here, a historic rivalry was born—as well as the career of one of the pillars of women's sports entertainment. With a big personality as well as a big elbow drop, Mae—alongside Mildred—took women's sports entertainment into new territories in the US throughout the 1940s. Her eye toward the future, Mae also trained new women to compete.

One of those athletes was The Fabulous Moolah. She trained with Mae and Mildred—and the expertise they imparted showed in her in-ring performances. In 1956, Moolah competed against 12 other women in a Battle Royal Match for the then-vacant

The Fabulous Moolah shows manager Harvey Wippleman who's the real Superstar— *SmackDown*, December 30, 1999.

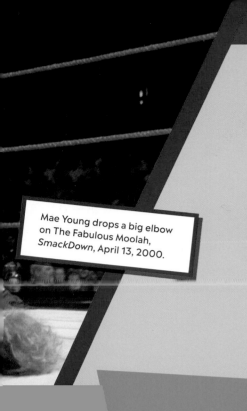

Women's Championship. Outlasting ten opponents, she finally eliminated Judy Grable, the high-flying "Barefoot Contessa," to win—and Moolah's astounding, 28-year reign as Women's Champion began.

All the while, Moolah trained new women Superstars. When she eventually lost her title in the 1980s, in one of the most-watched women's matches of all time, she moved into management, working with Superstar Leilani Kai, whom she had trained. Moolah helped set up the women's division in WWE and returned occasionally over the years to wrest the title from new hands. As "Spider Lady," she won her title back from Wendi Richter in 1985, and in 1999, in her seventies, she took it from the Superstar Ivory. She set new records, too, including becoming the first octogenarian to compete in WWE when she faced Victoria on her eightieth birthday.

True trailblazers like Mildred, Mae, and Moolah come along once in a lifetime. What was born with them would, over the following decades, evolve into something spectacular.

Mae Young drops a big elbow on The Fabulous Moolah, *SmackDown*, April 13, 2000.

> "We've got to give credit for everybody, from Mildred to Moolah to the Sherris to the Wendi Richters... Those are all different eras changing."
>
> —ALUNDRA BLAYZE

Judy Grable, "The Barefoot Contessa," makes sure that she's top of the heap!

Though this Superstar soared to rock star status, she began her career as a shy girl from Dallas. As a young talent, Richter got the opportunity to learn from the top names in sports entertainment. Before joining WWE, she trained with the some of the best, including The Fabulous Moolah, Leilani Kai, Joyce Grable, and Judy Martin. She even teamed up with a few: As part of a tag team called the "Texas Cowgirls," Richter and Grable took on Judy Martin and Velvet McIntyre, and she also battled alongside The Fabulous Moolah in early tag team matches.

So when Richter signed with WWE, she was ready to rumble. She teamed with Peggy Lee for a number of matches before befriending rocker Cyndi Lauper, who had become involved in sports entertainment. Her connection with the pop star ultimately created the "Rock 'n' Wrestling Connection," which catapulted Richter straight into main-event matches and WWE into the pop culture spotlight. Richter also became a two-time Women's Champion. Her first reign was cut short by Leilani Kai in *The War to Settle the Score*. She regained the title from Kai only to lose it to The Fabulous Moolah. Richter also continued to rock, making a memorable appearance in Lauper's music video for "She Bop."

Peggy Lee and Wendi Richter send Velvet McIntyre across the ring in a Tag Team Championship match, March 31, 1984.

WENDI RICHTER

A fiery Texan with a cutting-edge look and moves to match, Richter debuted in WWE in 1983 and quickly became the new face of women in sports entertainment.

> "One hundred fifty pounds of steel and sex appeal."
>
> —WENDI RICHTER

> "All I ever really wanted was respect."
>
> —WENDI RICHTER

Richter subjects the "Spider Lady" to some pain, in what turned out to be her final match.

ALONG CAME A SPIDER

Richter lost her title in 1985, in a controversial match against a mystery rival known only as the "Spider Lady." After a sketchy-at-best count-out, Richter unmasked her opponent to discover that she was none other than The Fabulous Moolah, whose reign Richter had ended to begin her own! Devastated by her defeat, Richter walked out of the arena and out of WWE for good, but with the satisfaction of knowing that she had changed WWE—and the way the world saw its female Superstars—forever.

THE BRAWL TO END

The *Brawl to End It All* kicked off on July 23, 1984, in Madison Square Garden in front of a capacity crowd. Although the event featured 11 matches and plenty of Superstars—including the Iron Sheik and Hogan—just one match aired on MTV: the Women's Championship Match.

After a fraught appearance on a Piper's Pit talk show segment in June 1984, Captain Lou Albano and rock star Cyndi Lauper set up a match to resolve their quarrel. They decided that each would train and manage a Superstar to battle on their behalf at *The Brawl to End It All* pay-per-view. In Lou's corner was Women's Champion The Fabulous Moolah, who had held the Women's Title for 27 years. In Cyndi's was new Superstar Wendi Richter.

Moolah covered her ears as Lauper and Richter entered the arena with Lauper's hit song "Girls Just Wanna Have Fun" blaring from the speakers. The match would be decided by one fall, with a one-hour time limit. Before the bell rang, Moolah attacked Lauper in her corner.

When the match started, Moolah landed the first blow with an arm drag and spun Richter right out of the ring. Tugging Richter around the ring by her hair, Moolah dominated the match until Richter landed a big punch that turned the tables. Richter managed to catch Moolah half in and half out of the ring, and seized the opportunity to flip her upside down. Moolah got so tangled in the ropes that not even Captain Lou could free the "Fabulous One." Even after the referee finally disentangled Moolah, she continued to take Richter's punishment: a full nelson, a suplex, a sidebreaker, a reverse chinlock, and even a punch from Lauper herself. Moolah landed a kick to Richter's midsection, followed by two backdrops. She pulled Richter up by her hair and flipped her into a double pin. The ref counted one, two... but at the last second Richter lifted her shoulder, effectively pinning Moolah underneath her, with both shoulders still on the mat. A new Women's Champion was crowned —as an irate Moolah released her aggression by drop-kicking the ref. The match was extremely popular with the WWE Universe, and became MTV's most-watched event—ever.

THE WAR TO SETTLE THE SCORE

Despite its name, the match at *The Brawl to End It All* didn't actually end the dispute. Moolah wasn't going to let go of her longtime title just like that, so she continued to challenge Richter. While Richter defended her title, Cyndi Lauper and Captain Lou eventually dropped their rivalry, with Lauper even giving Lou a gold record for helping her raise money for charity. Though Captain Lou and Lauper made up, there was still plenty of bad blood between Moolah and Richter (and Richter's manager, Lauper.) So in February 1985, a match was set for Richter to defend her title at another WWE–MTV event, *The War to Settle the Score*, against Moolah's charge, Leilani Kai. Kai defeated Richter thanks to interference by Moolah, setting up an exciting rematch to be held at the first-ever *WrestleMania*.

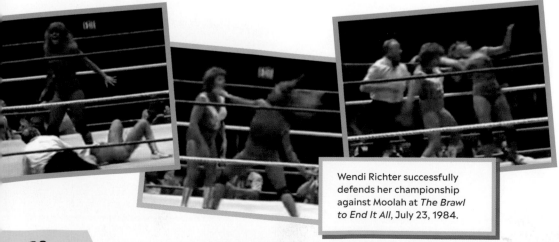

Wendi Richter successfully defends her championship against Moolah at *The Brawl to End It All*, July 23, 1984.

IT ALL

"I don't really have to say nothing because this belt right here says it all."

—WENDI RICHTER

"Right here is the new champ and a terrific symbol of the new woman."

—CYNDI LAUPER

Miss Elizabeth does her best to keep the formidable Mega Powers—"Macho Man" Randy Savage and Hulk Hogan—under control.

Miss Elizabeth managed "Macho Man" Randy Savage—and his outbursts—with impeccable grace and style. This was no mean feat, since she typically found herself in the middle of many of Savage's disagreements. She was a key connector in the super team-up of Savage and Hulk Hogan. As the "Mega Powers" tag team, the duo took on the "Mega Bucks"—Ted DiBiase and André the Giant—in the first-ever *SummerSlam* in 1988. No longer just Savage's beautiful sidekick, Elizabeth was now in control of two of the most celebrated Superstars in WWE at the time. Nonetheless, she wasn't averse to using the focus on her looks to her advantage: Elizabeth was key to the Mega Powers' victory at *SummerSlam* when, after the Mega Powers found themselves in trouble at the hands of the Mega Bucks, Miss Elizabeth gave everyone a mega surprise by ripping off her skirt to reveal her red underwear, distracting the Mega Bucks and allowing her team to get the win.

Miss Elizabeth and Hogan formed a tight friendship that would eventually break apart the Mega Powers, and Savage would replace Miss Elizabeth with Sensational Sherri at ringside. But years later, at *WrestleMania VII*, when Macho Man had been defeated in a Retirement Match against the Ultimate Warrior, Sherri turned on the already-down Savage. Miss Elizabeth intervened, manager and Macho Man were reunited, and the fans went wild.

MISS ELIZABETH

When "Macho Man" Randy Savage arrived in WWE in 1985, every manager in sports entertainment wanted to work with him. The woman who got the job became one of the most iconic ringside fixtures in WWE history.

The pair was on the same side again when Macho Man came out of retirement to win the WWE Championship at *WrestleMania VIII*.

Though Miss Elizabeth was ringside more than in the ring, she was front-and-center throughout WWE's first decade, and the history of sports entertainment wouldn't be the same without her steady presence.

> "She proved to everyone here tonight just how important she is."
>
> —COMMENTATOR GORILLA MONSOON

A RING IN THE RING

After an on-air proposal—where the Macho Man even got down on one knee—Miss Elizabeth and Randy Savage made it official during *SummerSlam 1991*, when they were married in a segment titled A Match Made in Heaven. Randy Savage walked down the "aisle" at Madison Square Garden wearing a gold-and-white top hat. Elizabeth then emerged, following the wedding party, in a satin and lace gown with a train worthy of royalty. The couple were pronounced husband and wife in front of the WWE Universe and the state of New York, and the Macho Man kissed his bride.

A blushing bride, Miss Elizabeth marries "Macho Man" Randy Savage during *SummerSlam 1991*.

Sherri muscles Debbi Combs into the turnbuckle.

This 2006 Hall of Fame inductee turned heads, first in the WWE women's division and then ringside as the manager of some of WWE's biggest Superstars. Sensational in the ring, she often resorted to any means necessary to defend her title. Startling all with her piercing scream, she battled her way to victory over Debbie Combs, Velvet McIntyre, and Desiree Peterson, among others. She won the Women's Championship, holding the title for 440 days, before losing it to Rockin' Robin on October 7, 1988.

When WWE temporarily dissolved the women's division in 1990, Sherri easily transitioned into a new role managing "Macho Man" Randy Savage. As a manager, Sherri was devious and didn't hesitate to distract Savage's competitors. She also amplified his energy and personality. No less sensational at ringside than in the ring, Sherri always sparkled in sequins or gold lamé fabric, and wore elaborate makeup. She cut a striking contrast to the more reserved Miss Elizabeth, with whom she had a bitter rivalry.

SENSATIONAL SHERRI

Sherri Martel's entrance into WWE was nothing less than sensational. In her first-ever match, she shocked all by besting her mentor, The Fabulous Moolah, and seized the Women's Championship in the process!

"She paved the way for a lot of others to follow."

—VINCE MCMAHON

When Sherri instigated a fight with Miss Elizabeth at *WrestleMania V*, tensions between former Mega Powers teammates Savage and Hulk Hogan exploded into bad blood that would last years. Sherri then attacked Savage in frustration, after his loss to the Ultimate Warrior in 1991, and their partnership dissolved.

Sensational Sherri held more monikers: "Sister Sherri," "Queen Sherri," "Scary Sherri," and "Sensuous Sherri." She also managed a range of top Superstars, including Ted DiBiase and Shawn Michaels. Sherri even sang Michaels' signature entrance music, "Sexy Boy," before she left WWE in 1993.

" I don't like you, and I don't care if you like me. "

—SENSATIONAL SHERRI

SENSATIONAL SURVIVOR

Sherri and The Fabulous Moolah drew lines, and the women Superstars declared their allegiances. This led to the women's division's first Elimination Match, which was scheduled as part of the first-ever *Survivor Series* on November 26, 1987, in Richfield, Ohio. Sherri lead Leilani Kai, Judy Martin, Dawn Marie, and Donna Christanello against Moolah and Velvet McIntyre, Rockin' Robin, Noriyo Tateno, and Itsuki Yamazaki. Moolah's team claimed victory when Tateno eliminated the last woman standing in Sherri's team, Judy Martin. Though the next women's *Survivor Series* matches wouldn't happen until 1995 and 2008, the seeds of an all-women *Survivor Series* were planted that night.

Sherri sensationally drops Rockin' Robin during the women's division's first-ever Elimination Match in 1987.

15

Sensational Sherri
Managed: Randy Savage, Ted DiBiase, Shawn Michaels

Miss Elizabeth
Managed: "Macho Man" Randy Savage, Hulk Hogan, Brutus Beefcake, "Hacksaw" Jim Duggan, Ric Flair

Stephanie McMahon
Managed: Triple H, Kurt Angle, Chris Jericho

AT THE RING'S EDGE

MANAGING SUPERSTARS

Female managers have worked with top names in WWE, including many male Superstars. These women have had a huge impact as the driving forces behind their charges' race to the top of their division. Miss Elizabeth and Sensational Sherri may have been the first to capture the spotlight and inspire many after them to manage, but several others will be remembered for shaking up sports entertainment.

Lana
Managed: Rusev

Carmella
Managed: Enzo Amore
& Big Cass, R-Truth

Terri Runnels
Managed: Goldust,
The Hardy Boyz,
Edge & Christian

Melina
Managed: MNM (Johnny
Nitro & Joey Mercury)

Ivory
Managed: D'Lo Brown,
Mark Henry

Jacqueline
Managed: Marc Mero

Trish Stratus
Managed: Test, Albert, Val Venis

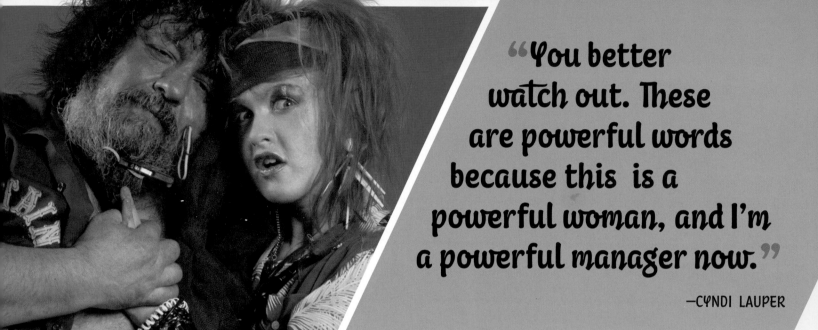

Captain Lou Albano and Cyndi Lauper's love-hate relationship formed some of the most pivotal moments for women in WWE.

> **"You better watch out. These are powerful words because this is a powerful woman, and I'm a powerful manager now."**
>
> —CYNDI LAUPER

Most people know Cyndi Lauper as the pop star hitmaker who created songs such as "She Bop," "True Colors," "Time After Time," and of course "Girls Just Want to Have Fun." But she also helped put women in sports entertainment in the spotlight.

Cyndi Lauper met legendary Superstar Captain Lou Albano on a plane. The two hit it off, and Cyndi later invited Capt. Lou to play the part of her dad in the music video for "Girls Just Want to Have Fun"— where she put him in a headlock.

When Cyndi appeared on Piper's Pit to be interviewed by "Rowdy"

Roddy Piper, Capt. Lou boasted that he was the one who'd discovered Cyndi, and that he was responsible for her success. "Tell 'em that no woman has ever accomplished anything without a man behind her," Capt. Lou told Cyndi. When Piper took Capt. Lou's side, Cyndi had had enough. She erupted, beating Capt. Lou with her purse and taking a swipe at Piper. To determine who was the better manager, Capt. Lou and Cyndi decided that they would settle the argument by picking a female competitor of their choice to manage.

A GOOD CONNECTION

And so the Rock 'n' Wrestling Connection was born. WWE even created a cartoon inspired by all

the action: *Hulk Hogan's Rock 'n' Wrestling.* Over the next few years, Cyndi and Capt. Lou squabbled and managed their respective Superstars in a series of high-profile bouts. They also set aside their differences and raised more than $4 million to help people with multiple sclerosis.

This collaboration between the worlds of pop music and sports entertainment led to many crossover opportunities, but its most lasting legacy was propelling the women's division into one of the most-watched women's matches of all time: Wendi Richter vs. The Fabulous Moolah in *The Brawl to End It All.*

Rock'n'roll meets WWE: Wendi Richter poses with WWE fan and Lauper's manager, David Wolff; Legend Hulk Hogan; Hollywood star Mr. T; and Cyndi Lauper.

CONNECTION

> ❝I am Wendi Richter's manager, and a manager sticks by her girl.❞
>
> —CYNDI LAUPER

Capt. Lou fends off a swat from Cyndi Lauper during a Piper's Pit segment on *Championship Wrestling*, June 16, 1984.

WRESTLEMANIA I

Kai and Richter's heated Women's Championship match was the only women's match in the first-ever *WrestleMania* and heralded the first of many key *'Mania* matches for female Superstars.

" [Wendi] has more Olympic ability in her little pinky than that Leilani Kai. "

—CYNDI LAUPER

Leilani Kai is in trouble as Wendi Richter whips her around at 1985's *WrestleMania I.*

As Wendi Richter bopped to the ring on March 31, 1985, with her manager Cyndi Lauper, Leilani Kai stood waiting in her trademark Hawaiian garb. Kai was seconded by The Fabulous Moolah, decked out in sparkling dollar-sign glasses made especially for the occasion. Even before the bell rang, the WWE Universe was prepared for fireworks. They were well aware of the bitter rivalry between Moolah and Lauper that had begun when Lauper managed Richter's successful bid to take Moolah's championship title in the summer of 1984.

Soon after the bell, the Superstars appeared to be evenly matched. But things escalated as loose hair, which had been pulled out, flew around the ring. Kai and Richter traded blows: a big right from Richter, a merciless boot from Kai. Kai's strategy seemed to be to not give Richter a breather—literally, because she even resorted to trying to choke Richter, right in front of the referee. As if that illegal move didn't show Kai's true colors—and give a hint of where she might have learned her win-at-any-cost strategy—

moments later, another would. As Kai maneuvered Richter to the ropes, Moolah took advantage. Seizing her opportunity, and Richter's hair, Moolah nearly dragged Richter out of the ring. She would have succeeded if it weren't for Lauper, who saved the day by finally loosening Richter from Moolah's grip.

A backbreaker maneuver from Kai nearly ended the match, but Richter hung on. Kai climbed to the top rope hoping to inflict a decisive blow; when she hit her target, it seemed inevitable she would pin her opponent. But somehow, Richter managed to flip out of Kai's grasp and roll her up for the win. With this thrilling victory, Richter began her second reign as Women's Champion.

Manager Cyndi Lauper and Superstar Wendi Richter celebrate their championship victory.

"I don't care what I gotta do or how I gotta do it to beat Wendi."

—LEILANI KAI

The Fabulous Moolah resorts to some sneaky interference in hopes of besting Wendi.

Hailing from Kawaguchi, Japan, Bull Nakano was a women's wrestling champion by the early age of sixteen. Before traveling to Mexico and eventually on to the US and WWE, Nakano cut her teeth in All Japan Women's Pro-Wrestling. There, she trained and regularly battled with Dump Matsumoto, Aja Kong, and Alundra Blayze. She would meet all of these future Superstars again when she entered WWE. Nakano's first WWE bout was in 1986, when she paired with Matsumoto to form the Devils of Japan. Matsumoto, dressed in full Japanese armor, and Nakano, with a half-shaved head, were a striking contrast to their opponents, Dawn Marie and Velvet McIntyre, who were dressed in sparkly, revealing costumes. Though Nakano and Matsumoto dominated most of the match, dragging McIntyre around the ring, the Devils of Japan lost. They would reappear throughout 1986, before returning to sports entertainment in Japan.

Nakano bends Alundra Blayze, her former opponent in All Japan Women's Pro-Wrestling, into a submission hold on *RAW*, January 14, 2005.

BULL NAKANO

Bull Nakano brought the intensity of Japanese wrestling to WWE. And with it, she also brought her intense in-ring presence—complete with striking hair and warpaint makeup.

" I grew up watching Bull Nakano, and she was amazing. "

—PAIGE

Nakano made a return to WWE in 1994, originally appearing with Luna Vachon. But Nakano was destined for something bigger. She embarked on a fierce rivalry with then Women's Champion, Alundra Blayze. Nakano grabbed the title from Blayze with a decisive Guillotine Legdrop at the Tokyo Dome in November 1994. Though Nakano would lose it again to Blayze five months later, her skill, character, and style helped breathe new life into the women's division.

Bull Nakano dazzles the WWE Universe with her flamboyant style and fierce attitude, SummerSlam. 29 August 1994.

STRAIGHT UP

Bull Nakano's signature ring style was as impressive as her ring presence. It evolved from tough but comparatively tame in her first WWE appearances, to hair-raisingly unique by her 1994 run. Nakano's dyed hair changed from a mohawk to what can only be called a mullet hawk. It was a style that—amazingly—stayed standing and survived most of her matches. With warpaint on her face and shoulder pads worthy of a general, Bull Nakano was one of the most elaborately dressed Superstars ever to grace the ring.

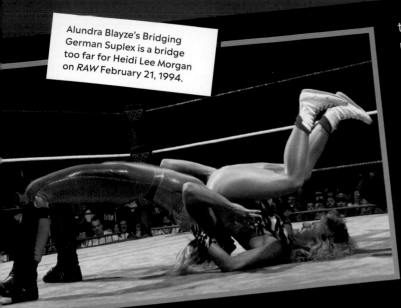

Alundra Blayze began her career in the American Wrestling Association in the mid-1980s. She then joined All Japan Women's Pro-Wrestling, where she took on future Superstars Wendi Richter, Sherri Martel, Bull Nakano, and Aja Kong long before they entered WWE.

When Blayze joined WWE in 1993, the Women's Championship had been vacant for three years, since Rockin' Robin's departure from the company. WWE decided to rebuild the women's division, starting with a six-woman tournament to decide the new champion. Blayze fired things up quickly, winning the tournament and title in December by defeating Heidi Lee Morgan with her signature Bridging German Suplex.

As Women's Champion, Alundra Blayze was eager for new blood in WWE's women's division. She requested that new Superstars be brought in to revitalize the competition. WWE agreed, and looked to Blayze's former stomping grounds, All Japan Women's Pro-Wrestling. There, among other competitors, they found a villainous bruiser with a unique style and ring presence: Bull Nakano. Bull would become Blayze's top competition in the women's division. Blayze reigned as champion for nearly a year, until Nakano took the title away in November 1994. It wasn't long before Blayze got it back, defeating Nakano during the April 3, 1995, episode of *RAW*. Blayze lost the title again to Bertha Faye (along with Harvey Wippleman). Not one to back down from a challenge, Blayze studied match tapes until she knew how to best Faye. When the two met again in a Championship Match, Blayze was victorious.

Blayze left WWE in 1994. The three-time Women's Champion holds a well-earned spot in the WWE Hall of Fame for the way she lit a fire in the women's division. She was inducted in 2015 by Natalya.

ALUNDRA BLAYZE

Before joining WWE, Blayze worked with Paul Heyman and "Ravishing" Rick Rude in WCW as the dangerous competitor Madusa. In these phenomenal training grounds, Blayze perfected her high-energy in-ring style.

> "She had that femininity, but she wasn't afraid to use stronger moves."
>
> —AJ LEE

> "I am the best ladies champion ever. Because when you see the Blayze, you're going to feel the heat."
>
> —ALUNDRA BLAYZE

Alundra Blayze, soon to become Madusa, drops the WWE Women's Title into the trash on WCW.

THE WOMEN'S TITLE IN THE TRASH

It was one of the most historic snubs in sports entertainment history. On December 18, 1995, Alundra Blayze, who had left WWE a few weeks earlier, appeared on rival company WCW's show. She appeared behind the announcers in a black leather suit. "This is the WWE Women's Championship belt," Blayze announced, holding the title up for the audience. Then she turned, picked up a nearby trash can, and dropped the title right into it. "And that's what I think of the WWE Women's Championship belt," she said. Blayze then confirmed she would be joining WCW and reassuming her former name, Madusa.

The move was decisive, and divisive. And it came at an uncertain time for women in WWE. In 1995, WWE had turned the company's focus away from the women's division. This fact, and the champion's actions, left the future of women Superstars in question.

WOMEN WITH ATTITUDE

In the mid-1990s, WWE was all about attitude. Beer-guzzling, crude Superstar Stone Cold Steve Austin regularly told off management. D-Generation X eagerly encouraged everyone to "Suck it!" The Rock "laid the smackdown" on "candy asses" everywhere. And Undertaker skulked the hallways, performing demonic deeds at will. It's here that the Divas division had its brazen beginnings. Not afraid to flaunt their stuff, show some skin, and battle in bikinis, ringside "Divas" soon worked their way inside the ropes. And when they did, competition heated up. High flying, power-kicking, super-strong women dazzled the WWE Universe. By the end of the Attitude Era, the women's division was marching toward revolution.

In 1995, a beautiful blonde woman walked down the ramp on the arm of WWE Superstar Skip. She was Sunny—Skip's manager and also part of Skip's tag team, the Bodydonnas, alongside his cousin Zip. Sunny's debut heralded the start of a new era defined by glamorous sidekicks with plenty of sass. Soon after Sunny came Marlena, Goldust's sexy, cigar-smoking manager. She sat ringside, propped in a director's chair to oversee Goldust's matches.

Just three months after Marlena's debut, brilliant blonde Sable arrived in WWE. She accompanied Triple H to the ring as his valet during *WrestleMania XII*. When Triple H mistreated her, Superstar Marc "Wildman" Mero saved the day. Sable was an instant hit as Mero's manager. And when Mero had to take some time off to rehab an injury, Sable found even more success solo—becoming more famous than the man she had managed.

Together with Jeff Jarrett's win-at-all-costs manager, Debra, the women who began ringside soon worked their way into plenty of drama, and sometimes the ring itself. Sable even eventually won the Women's Championship at *Survivor Series 1998*.

Although they competed more often in bikini contests than Battle Royals and hit poses more often than pins, these women of WWE were perfectly suited to the Attitude Era: They were sexy, sassy Superstars prepared to stop at nothing to get what they wanted. They could even be called... Divas!

THE DAWN OF THE DIVAS

"The more I get, the more I want."

—SUNNY

Sunny teases the WWE Universe before a match on *RAW*, February 27, 1997.

Marlena strides to the ring with the extravagant Superstar Goldust on *RAW*, June 23, 1997.

Miss Jackie gets thrown into the ring by Sable during a Playboy Evening Gown match at *WrestleMania XX*.

The ultimate Diva, Sable schemes her next move on *SmackDown*, May 27, 2003.

Victoria, Maria, Candice Michelle and Christy Hemme get ready for their Bikini Match on *RAW*, May 30, 2005.

Debra is ready for business on *RAW*, February 8, 1999.

Divas, Alicia Fox, Maryse, Jillan, Kelly Kelly, Eve, and Gail Kim battle in a Pyjama Pillow Fight on *RAW*, March 1, 2010

Jacqueline delivers a powerful kick to a cornered Sable on *RAW*, September 15, 1999.

Appearing on the June 1, 1998, episode of *RAW* on the arm of Sable's ex, Marc Mero, Jacqueline immediately made an enemy of the blonde bombshell. One of Jacqueline's early matches involved unconventional in-ring action: in an episode that was typical of the Attitude Era's more salacious moments, she was pitted against Sable in a bikini contest. Jacqueline won when Sable was disqualified for wearing nothing but paint.

This dominating Superstar proved she could offer much more to WWE than just her winning looks. During *RAW Is War* on September 21, 1998, Jacqueline defeated Sable (cruelly punctuating the win by cutting her rival's hair), to take the Women's Championship—and become the first African American to win the title. Although Sable regained the title at *Survivor Series*, Jacqueline would soon be on top again. But first, she formed Pretty Mean Sisters—or PMS—with Terri Runnels, aka Goldust's former manager, Marlena, and Ryan Shamrock. The Sisters didn't hesitate to resort to low blows and dubious tactics (faking pregnancies, among other tricks) to get their way. But it was only a matter of time before these big personalities had to go their separate ways.

JACQUELINE

It was never wise to mess with this Texan. As a former Women's Champion and Cruiserweight Champ, Jacqueline was a multifaceted and multitalented Superstar.

"**She kind of recreated what a champion looks like. It just really helped open the doors for women of all backgrounds, colors, sizes, shapes.**"

—ALICIA FOX

Jacqueline had another shot at the title when female Superstars drew straws to get their revenge on Harvey Wippleman, whom they felt had made a mockery of the Women's Championship when he disguised himself as a woman named Hervina. Wippleman arrogantly declared, "There's not a woman in the world who can beat me, because I'm a man." Jacqueline soon took the words right out of his mouth, repeatedly punching him and landing a big elbow before pinning him to end the match just seconds after the first bell. Jacqueline was inducted into WWE's Hall of Fame in 2016, kicking down another door in the process by becoming the first African American female inductee.

"**I can beat anyone— man or woman!**"

—JACQUELINE

THE FIRST AND ONLY (SO FAR)

During the May 4, 2004, episode of *SmackDown*, Chavo Guerrero challenged anyone he hadn't defeated before in WWE to take him on for his Cruiserweight Championship. To everyone's surprise, Jaqueline strode to the ring. As the WWE Universe chanted "Jackie, Jackie!" Chavo and his father, Chavo Guerrero, Sr., dissolved in peals of laughter. After mocking Jacqueline for more than a few minutes, Chavo concluded, "You don't really want to do this, do you, honey?" Jacqueline responded with a resounding smack.

Chavo had the weight advantage, but Jacqueline matched him in agility, landing a flurry of blows and dropkicks until Chavo caught her and slammed her to the mat. With the ref distracted by Guerrero Sr., Jacqueline felled Chavo with a low blow and wrapped him up, to become the first— and only—female Superstar to hold the WWE Cruiserweight Title.

Jacqueline responds to Chavo Guerrero's patronising comments with a well-aimed slap.

Specialty matches—bouts with hardcore rules or unique stipulations—amp the action up to truly spectacular levels. During WWE's edgier Attitude Era, female Superstars competed in some of the wildest and weirdest specialty matches in WWE.

Candice Michelle slides out of the tub in victory, leaving Melina gasping for breath.

EVENING GOWN MATCH

Sable vs. Jaqueline, September 14, 1998, *RAW*

A twist on the men's Tuxedo Match, an Evening Gown Match pits two dressed-to-the-nines Superstars against each other. The first to remove their opponent's gown wins. In this memorable match, Jaqueline, clad in a midnight blue gown, strode to the ring on the arm of Marc Mero. Sable arrived in a high-slit, high-necked black number. When the bell rang, Sable kicked off her heels, but Jacqueline kept hers on. The two locked up immediately, but the battle quickly turned into a clawing brawl.

Sable eventually outmaneuvered Jacqueline and perched on top of her. After knocking Jacqueline out with a Sable Bomb, Sable quickly shredded what was left of Jacqueline's gown. Following her win, Sable stripped anyway!

Jaqueline looks unperturbed about battling Sable in her evening gown.

CHOCOLATE PUDDING MATCH

Candice Michelle vs. Melina, June 3, 2007, *One Night Stand*

Though they may be considered gimmicks, some of the strangest matches can reveal true sports entertainment prowess. Candice Michelle and Melina displayed their skills when they tried to get a grip on each other in an extra-large kiddie pool filled to the brim with slippery chocolate pudding (complete with whipped cream and cherries on top).

The match was set to be decided by pinfall or submission. Melina cleverly donned a pair of goggles, but Candice evened things up by flipping her straight into the pudding. The two Superstars were quickly covered in liquid chocolate. Candice managed to slide out of the pool onto the floor, Melina close behind her. Somehow Candice was able to get enough traction to fold Melina into a pin, but Melina slid free and doled out a nasty shot to Candice's back. Melina tried to get Candice into a headlock, which proved impossible because of the slippery pudding. Candice grabbed hold and DDT'd Melina into the pudding with a spectacular splat. When Candice tried to drown her, Melina soon tapped out.

MATCHES

HAIR VS. HAIR MATCH

Molly Holly vs. Victoria, March 14, 2004, *WrestleMania XX*

Victoria was the Women's Title holder going into *WrestleMania XX*, but former champion Molly Holly wanted it back. The two would participate in a Hair vs. Hair Match for the honor. The stipulation of the match was that if challenger Molly Holly won, she would be crowned the new Women's Champion. If the challenger lost, however, her head would be shaved.

Molly dominated the first few minutes of the match, easily overpowering Victoria. But then an arm-ringer takedown backfired when Victoria was able to cartwheel out of it. Reenergized, Victoria landed some forceful body blows and a powerslam, until Molly bounced her off the rope. The two tussled on top of the turnbuckle until they tumbled off. Molly tried to execute a Widow's Peak, but Victoria did a quick backslide and pinned Molly for the win.

When it was time for her haircut, Molly took off running, but Victoria stunned her with a big hit and secured her in the barber's chair with restraints before gleefully shearing off all her lovely locks.

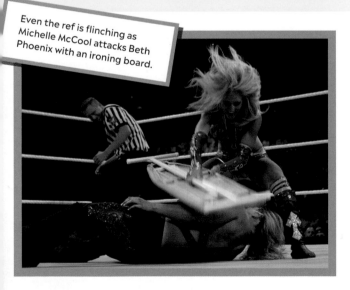

EXTREME MAKEOVER MATCH

Michelle McCool vs. Beth Phoenix, April 25, 2010, *Extreme Rules*

After months of avoiding a match-up with the "Glamazon" Beth Phoenix, then-Women's Champ Michelle McCool had to face her at *Extreme Rules*. Since Michelle was beauty-obsessed, the bout was an Extreme Makeover Match: Ringside was a table covered with makeup, mops, brooms, irons, and ironing boards—a buffet of beautifying products and domestic goods, to be used as the Superstars saw fit.

Two allies accompanied Michelle to the ring: Layla, the other half of their tag team duo LayCool, and LayCool's manager, Vickie Guerrero.

The match began, and Beth and Michelle quickly took the action out of the ring. As Beth took aim at Michelle, Layla interfered, swatting her with a broom. While Beth's back was turned, Michelle got her hands on some hairspray, which she spritzed straight into Beth's eyes. In the ring, Michelle dominated the blinded Beth, subjecting her to some unspeakable punishment with an ironing board. Attempting to make Beth submit, Michelle snapped her into a tight body scissors hold. But The Glamazon fought back, avoiding Michelle's attack with an iron and Vickie and Layla's double-team interference. Beth battled Michelle with a bucket and set up two ironing boards, but Vickie and Layla again intervened. They attacked Beth with a mop and broom, making her lose her balance and topple into the boards. Michelle made her move and set Beth up for her Faith Breaker maneuver—but the "Glamazon" countered and flipped Michelle into a Glam Slam for the win.

To quote the announce team, "Who would have thought that a Makeover Match could be so brutal?"

Strutting down the ramp to join D'Lo Brown and Mark Henry ringside on *RAW* in February 1999, Ivory seemed like just another beautiful sidekick. But she quickly interfered in their match against Owen Hart and Jeff Jarrett to secure their victory, and just as fast found herself in an impromptu scrap with their manager, Debra.

Ivory had a career in the ring as Tina Ferrari in GLOW (Gorgeous Ladies of Wrestling) before her WWE debut, and it wasn't long before she was competing again. She captured her first championship from Debra in her first year with the company.

Ivory wasn't quiet about what she thought of her fellow female Superstars, and broke the mold by competing in an evening gown rather than in typical ring attire. She was also quick to humiliate her elders—on the mic and in the

IVORY

Called a cornerstone of the Women's Evolution, Ivory began her career as a manager. But once she stepped into the ring, there was no denying her strength and skill.

"What she did here will always be part of this Women's Evolution."

—CHARLOTTE FLAIR

ring—when she relentlessly taunted and then took on The Fabulous Moolah and Mae Young when they reappeared on *RAW*. From her debut at the beginning of the Attitude Era, Ivory proved that women could be strong and opinionated, in addition to doing the work in the ring. As a three-time Women's Champion, she battled intimidating Superstars such as Lita and had a bitter rivalry with Chyna.

"This time you have a real champion. I don't just walk it, or talk it, or take it off. I just do it!"

—IVORY

BUTTONING IT UP

A backlash against all the attitude of the Attitude Era began in 2000. Forces both inside and outside of WWE began to protest the sexuality and violence they saw onscreen. The strongest voice in WWE was the "Right to Censor," a stable that included Steven Richards, Bull Buchanan, the Goodfather, Val Venis, and eventually Ivory. Ivory donned the RTC uniform: black slacks, white shirt, and sensible tie as she railed against her scantily clad competitors. She backed it up in the ring, crushing the competition until Chyna slowed her roll by defeating her in a Women's Title Match in *WrestleMania X-Seven*.

Ivory is supported by the "Right to Censor" members—The Goodfather, Val Venis, Bull Buchanan, and Steven Richards.

Chyna holds Shawn Michael's WWE Championship, alongside felow D-Generation X member, Triple H.

A woman so tough she was the bodyguard for a stable of five men, Chyna was a vital member of D-Generation X. Without her muscle—and regular interference—the team wouldn't have been the same. From the moment she debuted, attacking Goldust's manager, Marlena, ringside during a Triple H–Goldust match, the WWE Universe sensed Chyna was something special.

Her accomplishments include being the first woman to qualify for *King of the Ring*. She was the first woman to enter the *Royal Rumble*, not once, but twice. She was also the first—and only—woman to hold the Intercontinental Championship.

In addition to proving herself in the men's division, Chyna battled against some of WWE's most formidable female Superstars. Her main rivals included Lita, Trish Stratus, and Jacqueline. When she finally became Women's Champion, winning the title from Ivory at *WrestleMania X-Seven*, she did so with one of the most devastatingly smooth pins ever seen.

Harder to quantify than her in-ring accomplishments was Chyna's impact on the WWE Universe. Simply put, she was both awesome and inspiring. Chyna showed women—and men—everywhere that there's a place for strength in femininity. There's beauty in brawn. There's a place for the women among the men. And there's definitely a place for female powerhouses in WWE.

CHYNA
"THE NINTH WONDER OF THE WORLD"

A Superstar so spectacular that she earned a nickname akin to the "Eighth Wonder," André the Giant, Chyna shattered every convention for a woman in WWE on her arrival.

> "We wouldn't be where we're at or who we are without the contributions of the Ninth Wonder of the World."
>
> —SHAWN MICHAELS

A MATCH FOR THE MEN

Of course, Chyna was no shrinking violet. In the ring, backstage, or pretty much anywhere, she wouldn't hesitate to go nose-to-nose with the biggest male Superstars of her day. Chyna battled Jeff Jarrett with everything (including an actual kitchen sink) for the Intercontinental Championship. She heaved all 360-plus pounds of Mark Henry out of the Royal Rumble ring, clotheslined Val Venis, and she mopped the floor with Mankind. And woe to the male Superstar on the receiving end of one of Chyna's particularly vicious low blows.

Chyna sends Right to Censor's Val Venis reeling at *Armageddon*, December 10, 2000.

Trish Stratus began her WWE run managing the tag team duo Test and Albert, or team T&A, in 2000. Trish quickly went from supporting ringside to battling center stage when she joined T&A in the ring against The Hardy Boyz and Lita in Mixed Tag Team Matches. Trish and Lita then developed a rivalry of their own. In a Strap Match between the two Superstars, Trish came out on top and pinned Lita, thanks to interference by Stephanie McMahon. Trish's alliance with Stephanie would be short-lived, however. They frequently clashed over Trish's relationship with Stephanie's father, WWE Chairman Vince McMahon. Finally, at *No Way Out* in February 2001, Trish ended up covered in slop—the victim of a tag team attack from both Stephanie and Vince. Trish got revenge two months later at *WrestleMania X-Seven*, when she surprised Vince and his son Shane mid-match. After wheeling a sedated Linda McMahon, Vince's wife, to the ring, Trish slapped Vince and chased Stephanie from the arena.

That incident seemed to light Trish's fire, because she was on the championship track from then on. During *Survivor Series 2001*, she competed in a Six-Pack Challenge Match against Jacqueline, Lita, and Alliance representatives Ivory, Mighty Molly Holly, and Jazz. The Women's Title was on the line, with two Superstars starting in the ring and four more competitors waiting to tag-in at the corners.

After tossing Lita and Jazz through the ropes, Trish won by crushing Ivory with a devastating Stratusfaction maneuver. Trish went on to win the Women's Title six more times, defeating Victoria, Molly Holly, and finally Lita in her last match before retiring in 2006. Trish Stratus left with the title of "Diva of the Decade" and entered the WWE Hall of Fame in 2013.

Trish upends Jazz as Lita looks on during *Survivor Series 2001*.

TRISH STRATUS

With beauty, brains, and brawn, Trish Stratus is a fitness model turned WWE manager, seven-time Women's Champion, and Hall of Famer. Though her WWE career has been streaked with drama, she has always found a way to rise above it.

"Who wants some sweet Stratusfaction?"

—TRISH STRATUS

HARDCORE DIVA

Trish managed to get her hands on one of the hardest-fought titles in WWE history: the Hardcore Championship. In 2002, shortly after Trish lost the Women's Championship to Jazz, then–Hardcore Champion Steven Richards jumped into the ring to celebrate Jazz's victory. Under Hardcore rules, Richards's title could be defended at any time, as long as a referee was present. Bubba Ray Dudley took the opportunity to attack Stevie Richards. So with the aid of a table, trash can, and a Bubba Bomb move, Dudley defeated Richards to win the Hardcore Championship. Seeing an opportunity to take the title for herself, Trish then pinned Dudley to become Hardcore Champion—for a few minutes—until Dudley put her through a table and Stevie Richards pinned her, putting the title right back where it started. Minutes later, Raven appeared and took Dudley down with a sneak attack, pinning him to become the new Hardcore Champion. This was followed by a ruthless attack by Justin Credible, who became the new champ, followed by Crash Holly who pinned Credible for the title. When Bubba knocked Holly out with a trash can, Trish pinned Holly to become Hardcore Champion—for a few minutes—until Bubba put her through a table and Stevie Richards pinned her, putting the title right back where it started and ending the match. Nonetheless, Trish Stratus was one of a handful of women to hold this most extreme of titles.

Trish looks confident before her Women's Championship title loss to Jazz, RAW, May 6, 2002.

The story goes that Lita saw the energetic Superstar Rey Mysterio in an episode of *WCW Monday Nitro*, and she was hooked. Inspired by his acrobatic moves, she began to study wrestling and eventually moved to Mexico to train with luchadores.

When Lita made her WWE debut in 2000, it was alongside Essa Rios. While Lita didn't yet compete, she would practice Rios's high-flying moves after the match. The pair didn't last long: During a match with Matt Hardy, Rios knocked Lita off the apron, and as he checked on her, Hardy swooped in for the win. Rios blamed Lita for costing him the match, and their partnership dissolved when he powerbombed her.

That powerbomb paved the way for one of the most hardcore teamups in WWE history when Lita joined Matt and Jeff Hardy to form Team Xtreme. Team Xtreme regularly battled T&A (Test and Albert), and their bad blood set up a rivalry between Lita and T&A's manager, Trish Stratus, that would last throughout their respective WWE careers.

Lita won her first Women's Championship on the August 21, 2000, episode of *RAW.* In a match refereed by The Rock, Lita beat Stephanie McMahon when she landed her signature Moonsault for the win. It would be the first of her four reigns as Women's Champion.

Lita soars mid-Moonsault over a downed Trish Stratus on *SmackDown*, June 22, 2000.

LITA

Lita was all kinds of extreme: extremely tough, extremely beautiful, and extremely daring. Her high-flying Moonsaults were not for the faint of heart, and her edgy style and hardcore attitude set her apart.

"If it's not in your heart, you're not going to make it."

—LITA

Between 2002 and 2003, Lita was out due to a combination of injury and being fired by General Manager Eric Bischoff because she refused to bend to his will. When Lita returned to the company, she faced some hard times in the ring. She lost title matches to Victoria and Trish Stratus, and was stalked by the Superstar Kane. She was even forced to marry "The Big Red Monster" after a Till Death Do Us Part Match at *SummerSlam* 2005, though they would eventually divorce. Lita would go on to manage—and date and make out with—Edge, in some of the most censor-shocking moments in the whole of the Attitude Era. Through it all, Lita and Stratus maintained their bitter rivalry, with only an occasional truce. The result was some of the fiercest competitions between women ever seen in sports entertainment. Broken bones and torn muscles were regular occurrences. The only thing that could end their competition was retirement, which both of them did in 2006.

FLYING OVER BARRIERS

Beyond her shocking and boundary-breaking behavior in the ring with Edge, Lita constantly pushed the envelope as a competitor. She was fully in the action in the first-ever TLC Match, at *WrestleMania X-Seven*, featuring The Hardy Boyz vs. The Dudley Boyz vs. Edge and Christian. In fact, she was so involved that only a Spear from Edge could stop her.

Other career high points included: competing against Victoria in the first Women's Steel Cage Match on the November 24, 2003, episode of *RAW* and defeating Trish Stratus in the first women's main event match on *RAW*, on December 6, 2004.

Rhyno, an associate of Edge and Christian, tries to toss Lita as Spike Dudley slides in for a low blow at *WrestleMania X-Seven*.

Victoria hoists up her opponent Mickie James at *Unforgiven* 2004.

A former bodybuilder, Victoria was encouraged on her path to WWE Superstardom by none other than Chyna. She originally appeared as the head of the Godfather's female entourage, but made her in-ring debut in earnest in 2002 when she arrived ready to avenge wrongs she had suffered at Trish Stratus's hands when the two were fitness models. From then on, Victoria brought a truly obsessive and unhinged presence to the ring.

Victoria's matches were as intense as her personality. Her first title run came during her debut year, when she squared off against Trish Stratus at *SummerSlam* 2002 in the first-ever women's Hardcore Match—no disqualifications, no count-outs, fall count anywhere. After wielding a broom, a mirror, a rattan cane, an ironing board, a fire extinguisher, and multiple trash cans, Victoria was the victor.

Victoria also defeated Lita in the first-ever Women's Steel Cage match, and viciously shaved Molly Holly's head when she won a Hair Vs. Hair Match. She gained her second title in a Fatal 4-Way against Molly Holly, Lita, and Jazz when she flipped Molly over and pinned her in a backbend.

Between August 2005 and March 2006, Victoria was part of a villainous alliance with Candice Michelle and Torrie Wilson named Vince's Devils after WWE Chairman Vince McMahon. She later teamed up with newcomer Natalya.

Victoria retired in 2009, but not before changing the face of females in sports entertainment (by breaking a nose or two!).

VICTORIA

For women in WWE, there are four ways to break down barriers and enter uncharted territory: ignore those barriers, soar over them, fight through them, or smash them with a trash can. Victoria preferred the latter.

"I'll do anything to get my chance."

—VICTORIA

SHE'S MAKING A LIST, AND CHECKING IT TWICE...

Victoria would take on any Superstar who dared to stand in her way to glory. In fact, she had a checklist of opponents to ensure she ticked off every single one. Week after week, Victoria would stride to the ring, clipboard in hand, to battle another female Superstar. After meticulously checking each name off her list, leaving no one unharmed, she finally reached the last name: Women's Champion Mickie James. While Victoria couldn't grab the Women's Championship from James's grip, she sure did leave a trail of bruised and battered Superstars in her wake.

Victoria checks another victim off her list as she defeats Mickie James in a non-title match on *RAW*, December 18, 2006.

A TWIST OF FATE

THE FIRST WOMEN'S STEEL CAGE MATCH

The fickle turn of a roulette wheel gave Lita and Victoria the chance to make WWE history—and risk injury in a steel cage.

R AW General Manager Eric Bischoff clearly had a problem with Lita. He had fired her, but then changed his mind and decided to keep her around "to play with." The previous week, Lita's boyfriend, Matt Hardy, had broken up with her, and Bischoff was keen to pile on the agony.

A SPIN OF THE WHEEL

As Lita ran to the ring for her match with Victoria on the November 24, 2003, episode of *RAW*, Bischoff appeared on the jumbotron video screen. "Kill the music," he said. Bischoff, accompanied by Women's Champion Molly Holly, stood in front of a giant roulette wheel. On it, every possible match stipulation had been marked out—Falls Count Anywhere, First Blood, Last Man Standing, and other wild possibilities. A spin of the wheel would determine the evening's matches—and

Lita and Victoria's fate that night.

Molly Holly spun the wheel and it stopped on a Steel Cage Match. "I believe this is the first time in the history of *RAW* we've had two women in a Steel Cage Match," said Bischoff gleefully, and he and Molly Holly sarcastically wished Lita good luck.

As the cage was lowered over Lita, Victoria—famously a troubled soul—made her entrance. She gripped her head in her trademark, scary style, as if to quiet voices inside her mind.

BATTLE READY

Victoria had barely made it inside the cage, when Lita attacked, hurling her face-first into the unforgiving steel. Momentarily stunned, Victoria quickly regained her senses and bounced Lita off the mesh. Lita countered with a spinning sidewalk slam and headscissors. With Victoria sprawled on the mat, Lita began to climb the cage. She could win if she could climb out of the cage and jump to the floor. She had almost reached the top when Victoria caught up with her and pulled her down to the mat.

With a spin of a roulette wheel, Eric Bischoff and Molly Holly create the first women's Steel Cage Match.

Instead of escaping over the top of the cage, Lita spins into a Moonsault to take Victoria down.

"The cage is certainly taking its toll on both these female athletes!"

—COMMENTATOR JIM ROSS

The Superstars tussled until, with the crowd chanting her name, Lita landed a powerbomb on Victoria and started climbing the cage again. It looked like Lita was trying to escape, but instead she used her elevation to launch a soaring Moonsault, hoping to finish off her opponent.

AN EX'S INTERFERENCE

With victory in sight, Lita headed for the door. But as she lifted her foot to step out, her ex-boyfriend Matt Hardy appeared and slammed the door on her. Reeling, Lita fell back into the ring. As she writhed around in pain, Victoria crawled to the door and slid out, winning the match.

Lita viciously kicks Victoria from higher ground in the steel cage.

SEARCHING FOR A DIVA

The 2007 Diva Search contestants get ready to heat up the competition.

Diva Search challenges through the years: jousting in 2005; a competitive hot dog eating contest that same year; and a water fight in 2006.

I n 2003, WWE Diva Search was launched as an online talent contest. The WWE Universe voted for their favorite contestants online, and the company would make the final call on who would be chosen. The grand prize was a photo shoot in *WWE Magazine*. Out of a final four contestants, fitness expert Jamie Koeppe was crowned the first winner.

In its second year, WWE Diva Search got serious. This time, the winner would be awarded $250,000 and a contract with WWE. From a pool of thousands of applicants, 28 contestants were narrowed down for the casting special. There, an all-male panel that included Edge, Randy Orton, Triple H, and Chris Jericho narrowed the field further to the top ten.

The finalists appeared on *RAW*, competing against each other in a series of unconventional challenges—such as selling ice cream, smooching with Kamala, and eating pies. The "Diss the Diva" challenge was particularly memorable: The contestants had to berate each other (most of which had to be bleeped by censors).

A ROUTE TO THE TOP

Christy Hemme won the top spot that year, as well as the contract and the prize money. On the *RAW* roster, she quickly developed a rivalry with Trish Stratus and was trained by Stratus's archrival, Lita. Though Hemme won the Diva Search, the event yielded plenty of other talent: Michelle McCool, Candice Michelle,

and Maria Kanellis were among other Divas signed to WWE in 2004. Layla—who formed the formidable LayCool with Michelle McCool—was another Superstar who got her big break through Diva Search. She won the 2006 season, beating the Bella Twins and Maryse, among others.

The show was controversial, with some critics saying that it favored attractive contestants over trained professionals. However, there's no doubt that the program uncovered some of the biggest women Superstars of the Divas Era. WWE Diva Search ended in 2007. However, following the Revolution in WWE, a new version of the show was announced in 2019. It featured men and women, and was renamed the *WWE Superstar Search*.

Trish grips Lita in a painful chokehold in an attempt to force her to submit.

A MAIN-EVENT FIRST ON RAW

RAW, DECEMBER 6, 2004

Bad blood was simmering between Lita and Trish Stratus in the lead-up to their history-making main event match on *RAW*...

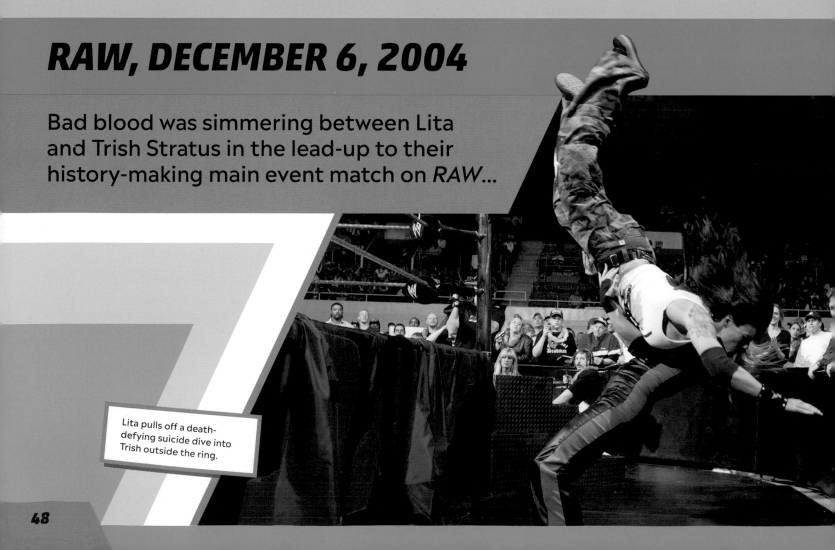

Lita pulls off a death-defying suicide dive into Trish outside the ring.

Lita and Trish Stratus's hostility grew when Trish taunted Lita for becoming pregnant with Kane's child. After Lita miscarried, she was ready for revenge. When the two Superstars faced off at *Survivor Series 2004*, Lita broke Trish's nose before being disqualified. The Women's Championship main event match at *RAW* would be the first time they had faced each other since then.

A HOMETOWN WELCOME

Reigning champion Trish strode to the ring first, a protective mask shielding her nose. That night, *RAW* was being held in Charlotte, North Carolina, so when Lita, a Carolinian, entered the stadium, she received the full support of the WWE Universe.

At the bell, the Superstars locked up and then traded blows and counters. Eventually, Trish was able to open up enough room to charge Lita, who alley-ooped her over the top rope with a big body drop. Having Trish sprawled on the ground outside the ring wasn't enough. Lita lined up, ran, and leaped into a soaring suicide dive. She landed badly on her chest and neck, and the arena fell silent while the referee checked on her.

UNMASKED

Incredibly, Lita got back on her feet and into the ring. Trish removed her mask—which, it turned out, she didn't need—and used it to bat Lita. The Superstars tussled, with Trish ending up on the top turnbuckle, snaring Lita with a chokehold. Lita countered by snapping Trish to the mat.

With the crowd chanting her name, Lita executed a huge Superplex from the top turnbuckle that had both Superstars out for three counts. Lita was able to cover Trish, but Trish quickly got a shoulder up.

TWIST OF FATE

The evenly matched opponents continued to battle, dealing out moves and counters: Trish punched Lita on the turnbuckle, and Lita countered with a powerbomb. She rolled Trish up, but Trish evaded the count. Trish landed a big DDT and almost got the count on Lita, but not quite. Trish then lined up for a signature Stratusfaction move, but Lita countered.

The tide didn't turn one way or the other until Lita caught Trish by the hair and turned her into a Twist of Fate. With Trish lying dazed on the ground, Lita finished with a big Moonsault and finally got the three count for victory.

Lita was crowned the new Women's Champion—and with such a thrilling, hard-fought battle, she and Trish had proved that women were well worth the main event on *RAW*.

> "I can't believe the effort, the heart both women displayed..."
>
> —COMMENTATOR JIM ROSS

Victorious in her home state of North Carolina, Lita proudly shows off her title to the WWE Universe.

Mickie pulls on Trish's injured knee to weaken her and increase her chances in the match.

FROM IDOL TO RIVAL

TRISH STRATUS VS. MICKIE JAMES, WOMEN'S CHAMPIONSHIP MATCH, WRESTLEMANIA 22

On the October 10, 2005, episode of *RAW*, Trish Stratus had been knocked down in a match against Victoria. Suddenly, an ecstatic mystery fan skipped to the ring to rescue her. Mickie James had made her debut. But what began as fan-worship quickly turned to an uncomfortable obsession, and Mickie James revealed herself to be more Trish's stalker than supporter. This strange situation came to a head on *RAW* in March, 2006. Ahead of *WrestleMania 22*, Mickie presented Trish with a present. In the ring was a gift box the size of Big Show. Inside was Trish's friend, Ashley Massaro, bound and gagged.

THE SHOWDOWN

When the bell rang on their match for the Women's Championship at *WrestleMania 22*, Trish came out fists flying and ready for revenge. She had the upper hand, until she went for a high kick and connected with the steel ring post rather than Mickie. And that's when Mickie seized the opportunity to decommission Trish's left leg one blow at a time.

Mickie landed a low dropkick and a punishing move to Trish's already injured knee, and Trish was flagging. The crowd began chanting for Mickie—and she reveled in the adulation. Responding to the fans' energy, Mickie strung Trish up on the ropes and came down hard again on the back of her knee. Trish rebounded with two clotheslines and then slammed Mickie to the mat. She even hit a running powerbomb, but nothing could keep Mickie down.

In the end, Mickie countered Trish's Stratusfaction move and Trish's legs started to buckle. Mickie gave Trish one swift high kick, and Trish hit the mat. By the count of three, Mickie James was the new Women's Champion. And the WWE Universe experienced one heck of a *WrestleMania* moment.

"You love me now, Trish Stratus?"

—MICKIE JAMES

Mickie James celebrates winning the Women's Championship In a decisive victory.

Trish slams Mickie to the mat, momentarily slowing Mickie's rampage.

51

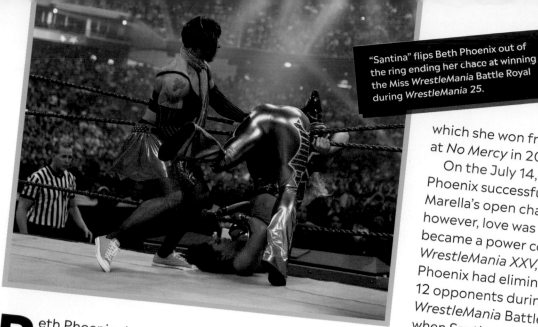

"Santina" flips Beth Phoenix out of the ring ending her chace at winning the Miss WrestleMania Battle Royal during WrestleMania 25.

Beth Phoenix always dazzled. Growing up in upstate New York, Phoenix set her sights on wrestling early. She was kicking down doors in high school, becoming the first female on the otherwise all-male wrestling team. After college, Phoenix was ready for the ring. When she appeared on her first episode of *RAW* on May 8, 2006, she was Trish Stratus's mysterious ally, assaulting Mickie James. However, their alliance didn't last long: On the June 5 episode of *RAW*, Victoria broke Phoenix's jaw during a brutal match, and though Phoenix won the bout, she needed medical leave and surgery to repair her face. When she returned to the ring, "The Glamazon" dominated and battled for the Women's Championship,

which she won from Candice Michelle at *No Mercy* in 2007.

On the July 14, 2008 episode of *RAW*, Phoenix successfully answered Santino Marella's open challenge to WWE Superstars; however, love was the real winner. "Glamarella" became a power couple in WWE until *WrestleMania XXV*, April 5, 2009. Phoenix had eliminated a record 12 opponents during the Miss *WrestleMania* Battle Royal Match when Santino, masquerading in drag as "Santina," ousted her!

Ultimately, the WWE management just couldn't handle The Glamazon, and Phoenix was summarily fired by *RAW* General Manager Vickie Guerrero in 2012 for "poor performance" when defeating AJ Lee.

Inducted into the Hall of Fame in 2017, Phoenix returned to WWE in 2018—in the relative safety of the announce table. She's currently a commentator for NXT, though she has been coaxed into the ring on occasion. At 2019's *Wrestlemania 35*, she reunited with her friend Natalya to challenge for the WWE Women's Tag Team Championships, narrowly losing to the Ilconics (Billie Kay and Peyton Royce).

BETH PHOENIX
"THE GLAMAZON"

She's The Glamazon who turned heads and then slammed bodies. She'd take on male Superstars and win, or she'd terrorize female rivals two at a time and send them crashing to the mat.

"**There is no one who can match my power.**"

—BETH PHOENIX

> "**The perfect combination of strength and beauty.**"
>
> —BETH PHOENIX

Beth Phoenix muscles Melina and Mickie James up onto her back during *Judgment Day 2008*.

FEATS OF STRENGTH

Handing out Glam Slams like candy? Sure thing. Double-slamming two Superstars at the same time? No problem. Pulling The Great Khali's gigantic frame over her shoulder and out of the Royal Rumble? Nothing to it. Beth Phoenix's power was undeniable, and regularly on display. Few feats of strength proved her superhuman abilities better than when Phoenix would rack up her Superstar rivals in spectacular double moves. A perfect example of this occurred during the Women's Championship Triple Threat Match at *Judgment Day 2008*. The Glamazon stacked Mickie James on top of Melina and issued a double backbreaker to both at the same time.

Vickie Guerrero's time in WWE is marked equally by tragedy and triumph. She debuted in 2005 alongside her husband, Eddie Guerrero, and her friend Rey Mysterio. Vickie inserted herself into their fight about Mysterio's son, Dominick, attempting to keep the peace. She even interfered during their Ladder Match to determine custody of the child, accidentally knocking Eddie from the ladder and costing him the win.

A few months later, Eddie passed away. He was inducted into the WWE Hall of Fame shortly after, and a heartbroken Vickie accepted the honor on his behalf. When Vickie returned to the ring it was with her nephew, Chavo Guerrero. Embroiled in bad blood between Chavo and Rey Mysterio, Vickie ultimately sided with family and turned her back on her friend.

Vickie's first taste of corporate life came when she took a job as an assistant to *SmackDown* General Manager Teddy Long in 2007. After Long had a heart attack, Mr. McMahon promoted Vickie to the role of General Manager. Ever the cunning one, Vickie wielded her power to her (and her friends') advantage. It was quickly discovered that Vickie and the Superstar Edge had a secret relationship, and the new GM was setting matches in his favor. Undertaker didn't take kindly to this, and hit her with a Tombstone at *Survivor Series 2007*.

When Vickie returned to WWE, it was in a wheelchair and with vengeance on her mind. She formed La Familia, a stable with Chavo, Edge, Curt Hawkins, and Zack Ryder, leading them as their matriarch. Vickie's power knew no bounds. Thanks in no small part to her GM

privileges and her blatant interference in matches, Edge reigned as World Heavyweight Champion for over two months. Vickie even wielded her authority to banish Edge's rival Undertaker from WWE. She would eventually rise to become GM of *RAW* as well as *SmackDown*, and her signature scream, "Excuse me!" rang through the halls of both brands, until April 6, 2009, when she decided to focus solely on *RAW*.

While Vickie could pull all the strings in her job, she had less control over her love life. Her marriage to Edge crumbled because of infidelity on both sides. After Edge admitted that he'd used Vickie to climb the ladder to a championship, Vickie had a breakdown and took a leave of absence.

La Familia—Curt Hawkins, Edge, Vickie Guerrero, Chavo Guerrero, and Zach Ryder—celebrates a victory, ECW, February 1, 2008.

VICKIE GUERRERO

She doesn't have McMahon as her last name, but few people have made more of an impact on the sports entertainment business than Vickie Guerrero.

" I'm not here to prove myself to anyone. "

—VICKIE GUERRERO

HARD BUT UNFAIR

Vickie returned to WWE as a special consultant for *SmackDown* in 2009 and teamed up with LayCool, aka the duo of Michelle McCool and Layla. Participating in heated rivalries in the women's division, Vickie even occasionally ended up competing in the ring. She also managed Dolph Ziggler, and, with her insight and coaching, helped him to achieve a stint as World Heavyweight Champion. Vickie held several prominent positions in the company. She was fired as *RAW* GM following a job evaluation by both Stephanie McMahon and the WWE Universe, who were given the chance to vote online on her job performance. Mr. McMahon rehired her as *SmackDown* GM, a post she held until a very messy, career-ending Chocolate Pudding Match with Stephanie on *RAW*, June 23, 2014.

Vickie Guerrero never hesitated to meddle, interfere, or arrange matters to her and her allies' advantage. But during her time as a WWE General Manager, she certainly didn't let a single ounce of her power go to waste!

Vickie finds herself covered in chocolate pudding after her match with Stephanie McMahon.

FIRST AT THE TABLE

THE FIRST TAG TEAM TLC MATCH, BETH AND NATALYA VS. LAYCOOL, TLC 2010

Natalya and Beth lift Layla as her partner, Michelle McCool, kicks to try to set her free.

Friends Layla and Michelle McCool, members of LayCool, were a talented tag team—and total trouble. The team dominated the women's division in 2010. But when "Glamazon" Beth Phoenix and the Women's Champion Natalya formed a tag team, the competition leveled up. During *TLC 2010* the four Superstars would meet in the first-ever women's Tag Team Tables Match.

THE ONLY WAY OUT IS THROUGH—A TABLE!

Set up outside the ring were two tables—one standard issue and one table that Beth and Natalya had painted pink and covered in an unflattering caricature of LayCool. Inside the ring, the Superstars faced off. To win the match, at least one Superstar would have to put an opponent through one of the tables. To start things off, Natalya and Beth each bodyslammed one member of LayCool. While Layla and Michelle lay dazed on the mat, Beth and Natalya went to work setting up their special pink table inside the ring. The Glamazon piled both Superstars onto her shoulders in a double fireman carry and headed toward the table, but LayCool slipped out of her crushing grasp and fought back.

After tossing Beth out of the ring—via a slam to the ribs and a painful-looking fall—LayCool worked Natalya over with body blows. As LayCool set Natalya up for what looked like it could be a match-ending Faith Breaker, Beth—now back on her feet—intervened. In another show of her phenomenal athleticism, Beth pressed Michelle above her head, but Layla came to the rescue. When Beth and Natalya held Layla over a table, Michelle returned the favor by quickly moving it out of reach and kicking Natalya in the back.

Natalya grabbed Michelle and slammed her back to the mat. Layla tried to intervene—but she ended up on top of Michelle. No one in the audience missed the glint in Natalya's eye as she decided to go for the double Sharpshooter. Michelle, in horrendous pain, tried to tap out, but the only way out of a tables match is through a table.

I'M SO READY FOR THIS

Beth set up the pink table, and she and Natalya embraced, shouting "I'm so ready for this!"—but LayCool still had some oomph left. Kicking their way out of the Divas' hands, they dumped Beth out of the ring again. Double-teaming Natalya, they perched her atop the turnbuckle and set her and the table up for a double suplex. But Beth intervened again. Natalya dazed LayCool with strategic blows before pushing both of them, simultaneously, off the ropes and onto the table. Amazingly, the table didn't break completely, so the match wasn't over—yet. Natalya got to her feet and set sail, splashing LayCool straight through the table. Beth and Natalya were victorious.

Natalya dives and smashes LayCool through the table for the win.

Beth and Natalya are declared the winners as LayCool lie dazed behind them.

DOUBLE TROUBLE

The first women of WWE formed some of the most dynamic team-ups in their division. The Women's Tag Team Championship was retired in the late 1980s, but when the new Women's Tag Team Title was introduced in 2019, many strong competitors were ready to take up the mantle.

THE JUMPING BOMB ANGELS

Itsuki Yamazaki and Noriyo Tateno joined forces as the Jumping Bomb Angels in 1981. Showing their strength as a team during *Survivor Series 1987*, they were the last women standing in a massive match that included The Fabulous Moolah, Rockin' Robin, and Sensational Sherri. They nabbed the Women's Tag Team Championship from the dominating team, the Glamour Girls, in a well-fought, Two-Out-of-Three Falls Match in 1988.

THE GLAMOUR GIRLS

Glittering in gold, the Glamour Girls—Leilani Kai and Judy Martin—sparkled during the 1980s in the women's division's early tag team matches. Managed by Jimmy Hart, the Girls reigned as Women's Tag Team Champions twice, for a combined 1,888 days, in 1985 and 1988.

THE CHICKBUSTERS

During the Divas Era, when there was no Women's Tag Team Championship, AJ Lee and Kaitlyn formed a duo as The Chickbusters. They showed their prowess in multiple-Superstar bouts by winning a Six-on-Six Tag Team Match, followed by a Seven-on-Seven Tag Team Match. However, their friendship faded and they went from teammates to rivals.

LAYCOOL

Tight friends Layla and Michelle McCool became "LayCool," and terrorized the women's division, making mean-spirited remarks about other Superstars from their debut in July 2009 to their breakup in May 2011. These best friends even became "co-champions" when they teamed up to defeat Beth Phoenix in a Handicap Championship Match on *SmackDown* in May 2010.

THE BELLA TWINS

Had the Women's Tag Team Title been available between 2008 and 2015, there's little doubt The Bellas would have owned it. They debuted as a tag team on *SmackDown*, November 21, 2008, defeating Natalya and Victoria. Nikki and Brie Bella always had each other's backs, confusing rivals, such as Jillian Hall, Eve Torres, and Paige, with "Twin magic."

THE BOSS 'N' HUG CONNECTION

Whether they're friends or not, Sasha Banks and Bayley are two of the hardest-working women in WWE. So when they *are* on the same page—and on the same team—they reign supreme. Working together as the Boss 'n' Hug Connection, they defeated Absolution stable's Sonya Deville and Mandy Rose at *Elimination Chamber 2019* to become the first-ever WWE Women's Tag Team Champions.

Stephanie McMahon has the power and she's not afraid to use it. She got her start in WWE modeling t-shirts for a merchandise catalog. Since then, she's worked her way up to the highest ranks in the company as Chief Brand Officer of WWE. Stephanie has also done her fair share of ring time. In her early matches she was coached (and assisted) ringside by Triple H and D-Generation X. Since then, she has battled her way through the women's division: Sable, Lita, Jaqueline, Trish Stratus, Brie Bella, and Ronda Rousey have all squared off with Stephanie at some point. She's even held the Women's Championship, winning it from Jacqueline on the March 30, 2000, episode of SmackDown (with a little help from her D-Generation X friends, of course).

Over the years, Stephanie has challenged her WWE Chairman father many times, including battling him in an I Quit Match and protesting against his dalliances with Trish Stratus and Sable. She's also threatened his power as part of The Alliance with her brother, Shane.

Together with her husband, Triple H, Stephanie formed The Authority in 2013. Originally intended to prevent Daniel Bryan from becoming WWE's biggest Superstar and install Randy Orton as the top talent, The Authority ruled WWE for three years.

Stephanie introduces Triple H at *WrestleMania* 32, before his match with Roman Reigns.

STEPHANIE MCMAHON
"THE QUEEN OF WWE"

This McMahon is as game for the boardroom as she is for the ring. She's sparred with Superstars, beaten champions, and even taken on her own dad, WWE Chairman Mr. McMahon!

> **"The legacy that WWE leaves behind rests on my shoulders."**
>
> —STEPHANIE MCMAHON

Stephanie talks business with her brother, Shane McMahon, and father, Vince McMahon, on *RAW*, February 22, 2016.

POWER AND RESPECT

There's no doubt Stephanie has inherited the vision, the business acumen, and sometimes the vindictiveness of her father—in fact, she's fired several Superstars in the same humiliating fashion as he does. Stephanie also cites her mother, Linda McMahon, as a role model in life and in business. Thanks to Mrs. McMahon, Stephanie says, "I never saw gender as a barrier." The women's division has evolved in no small part due to Stephanie's interest and investment in it. Setting the Divas Revolution in motion, supporting ground-breaking ventures such as NXT, and advocating for women-first, women-focused, and women-only events, Stephanie McMahon wants to ensure that the women's division is just as high profile as the men's.

EVOLVING

The essential elements for the next stage of "Women's Evolution" were brewing by 2010. As Superstars such as CM Punk and John Cena hit new peaks of popularity, crossover sensation and total "Beast" Brock Lesnar was just starting to slam his way to Suplex City. Over the course of the next decade and beyond, championships traded from top dog Randy Orton to underdog Daniel Bryan and back again. Groups such as The Shield and The New Day energized the WWE Universe. And, as ever, The Authority's power was put to the test. Behind the excitement of the main brands, WWE welcomed a new addition: NXT, originally a reality show, began training and debuting talent.

It was against this exciting backdrop that WWE's women's division—built on the shoulders of all the women who came before—began to rapidly evolve. Women Superstars racked up firsts and busted through barriers, raising their profiles and establishing fresh images of charisma and in-ring athleticism. With the full support and enthusiasm of the WWE Universe, and with Triple H and Stephanie McMahon in their corner, the women Superstars in sports entertainment seemed to be on a trajectory that was heading just one way: up!

Team Total Divas celebrate their win over Team B.A.D. & Blonde at the *WrestleMania 32* Kickoff show.

The first time the WWE Universe saw The Bella Twins was in the 2006 Diva Search competition. They didn't win the contest—but that was one of the few times in their WWE careers that The Bella Twins didn't steal the show. With a little bit of "Twin Magic," there was almost nothing the twins couldn't do. Together, they managed Superstar Daniel Bryan, appeared on the all-women season of NXT, dazzled in *Total Divas*, and also had their own reality TV show, *Total Bellas*. Apart, Brie battled management when she got entangled in Bryan's business against the McMahons and was forced to quit WWE, though she was soon rehired. She led Team Total Divas to victory in a 10-Superstar Tag Team Match in the *WrestleMania 32* Kickoff show. And Nikki was declared "The Face of the Divas Division" by the McMahons.

Each Bella Twin won the Divas Championship with a little help from the other. Brie reigned for 70 days, while Nikki's second reign lasted for a remarkable 301 days—surpassing AJ Lee's reign and making Nikki the longest-reigning Divas Champion in history. Brie and Nikki shook things up in the men's division, too, leaving a trail of heartsick male Superstars competing for their affections. Of course, the twins came into the world as a pre-made tag team, but when Alicia Fox joined them, Team Bella's rule over the division became the catalyst for the Divas Revolution in 2015, when NXT Superstars teamed up with WWE Superstars to try to take them down.

The twins have effectively been retired since 2016—both for family reasons and to broaden their scope in entertainment and business. However, they briefly returned in 2019 to WWE to support and then attack *RAW* Women's Champion Ronda Rousey.

THE BELLA TWINS

Together and apart, Brie and Nikki were major players in the late Divas Era. Without The Bella Twins and their unexpected alliances, stormy disputes, and momentous title reigns, would there have been a Divas Revolution?

"We can kick anyone's butt in the ring."

—BRIE BELLA

> "We are dominant."
> —NIKKI BELLA

SEEING DOUBLE

Brie Bella debuted on *SmackDown* in August 2008 solo—or so the WWE Universe thought. Whenever she was winded during a match, Brie would scoot under the ring and reappear refreshed. The move helped her win countless bouts. That is, until Natalya and Victoria uncovered the secret of "Twin Magic." When Brie escaped under the ring, the two Superstars went after her. Each emerged from the ring skirt with a Bella in hand, revealing that Brie and Nikki were working together. The amazing revitalization Brie experienced during her matches was really a Superstar switcheroo!

Victoria and Natalya expose the secret of "Twin Magic" when they each pull a Bella out form under the ring.

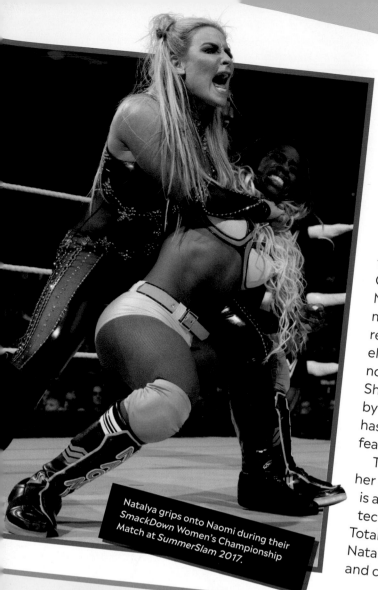

Natalya grips onto Naomi during their *SmackDown* Women's Championship Match at *SummerSlam 2017*.

As the daughter of Jim "the Anvil" Neidhart and niece of Bret "Hit Man" Hart, Natalya has sports entertainment running in her veins. She was the first woman ever to train in the Hart family's "Dungeon." Natalya first appeared on *SmackDown* in April 2008, when she helped Victoria survive an attack by Michelle McCool and Cherry. In her first official match, she bulldozed Cherry and forced her to tap out of a vicious Sharpshooter.

After a stint in ECW, she joined the Hart Dynasty, a formidable tag team trio, in 2009. Later, she also teamed up with "The Glamazon," Beth Phoenix, to form the Divas of Doom tag team. Natalya's grit and tenacity made her a perfect teammate in any massive multi-Superstar tag team match or battle royal, but her real glory was as a singles Superstar. While the Divas Championship eluded her for a few years, by *Survivor Series 2010*, she had defeated not one but two Divas—Layla and Michelle McCool—for the title. She would later become *SmackDown* Women's Champion in 2017 by defeating Naomi at *Summerslam*. This multitalented Superstar has also done stints as a manager, a coach, and of course, she's featured on the *Total Divas* reality show.

Though her methods are sometimes questionable and her alliances shifty, no one can deny that the "Queen of Harts" is a tough technical competitor who brings the Harts' trademark technical abilities—and famous Sharpshooter move—to the ring. Total Superstar submission is her mission. In every match, Natalya proves that she can do right by her family legacy and carry it forward while forging her own path.

NATALYA
"QUEEN OF HARTS"

This third-generation Hart Family Dynasty member is taking her family name somewhere it's never been before: into women's sports entertainment history.

> **"When you mess with the best, you go down with the rest."**
>
> —NATLAYA

Natalya, Tyson Kidd, and David Hart Smith amp up the crowd before their match at *Bragging Rights 2009*.

ALL IN THE FAMILY

The Hart Dynasty consisted of Natalya, her husband, Tyson Kidd, and her cousin David Hart Smith. The three of them won a 4-Superstar Tag Team Match at *Bragging Rights 2009*. They also took on The Usos and Tamina—all members of multi-generational sports entertainment families—in a sports entertainment legacy battle, facing off in mixed tag team matches. Natalya won the match by pinning Tamina when both sides faced off at *Fatal 4-Way 2010*. Fiercely protective of the family name, whenever the Hart family or the Hart family legacy needed defending, Natalya and the Hart Dynasty were there—including the time when Bret Hart took on Mr. McMahon during *WrestleMania XXVI*.

MATRIARCHS

Many of the Superstars of sports entertainment wouldn't be where they are today without the strong women who were the backbone of their family. Here are some of the matriarchs who have sustained generations of Superstars.

Helen Smith makes sure her son Bret "The Hit Man" Hart is well-fed and ready for the ring.

"Growing up, we didn't have a sandbox in our backyard. We had a wrestling ring."

—NATALYA

HELEN HART

When Helen Smith met Canadian Stu Hart in New York City, a sports entertainment dynasty that would span decades began. Married in 1947, Stu and Helen would go on to have 12 children, among them Bret and Owen Hart. Matriarch Helen helped Stu keep the Hart Family Dungeon —in which countless Superstars trained—running, and even occasionally appeared in WWE storylines involving the family.

Helen dons Bret's trademark shades as she sits ringside at *In Your House 16: Canadian Stampede*.

> **"She kept the business going... It was tough."**
>
> —THE ROCK ON HIS GRANDMOTHER LIA

The Rock's grandmother, Lia shares a smile

The Rock's mother, Ata, Lia Maivia, and a young Dwayne Johnson pose for a family photo.

LIA MAIVIA

Following the death of her Superstar husband, High Chief Peter Maivia, The Rock's grandmother Lia became one of the first women promoters in sports entertainment, taking control of NWA's Polynesian Pro Wrestling in the 1980s.

> **"I saw my mom as a CEO and never thought there wasn't an opportunity to be a CEO."**
>
> —STEPHANIE MCMAHON

LINDA MCMAHON

Mr. McMahon's wife, Linda, helped found WWE and was CEO until 2009, when she turned her talents to politics and government. She also stepped in front of the WWE camera on occasion. At *WrestleMania* 2000, she was in Mick Foley's corner for the main event match.

Linda McMahon addresses the WWE Universe.

Linda McMahon gives Mr. McMahon a talking to on *RAW* April 9, 2001

The *Total Divas* season 7 cast on the ropes: (clockwise from top left) Lana, Nia Jax, Carmella, Alexa Bliss, Nikki Bella, Natalya, Brie Bella, and Maryse, with Naomi in the center.

TOTAL DIVAS

BECOMING REALITY SUPERSTARS

The *Total Divas* reality TV show follows WWE Superstars' eventful professional and personal lives, from ringside to backstage and even inside their very own homes. The first season aired in 2013 and was been nominated three times for the Teen Choice Awards and the hit program shows no signs of stopping.

The original *Total Divas* cast featured Natalya, Naomi, the Bella Twins, Eva Marie, and JoJo. Later seasons brought Alicia Fox, Paige, Summer Rae, Mandy Rose, Alexa Bliss, Nia Jax, and more. And of course the show features plenty of cameos from male Superstars such as Brie Bella's husband, Daniel Bryan, John Cena, and the ever-hilarious Titus O'Neil.

As the hit show follows the Divas through training for high-stakes matches and organizing their home life, there are plenty of crazy antics: a somersaulting Brie Bella in "Brie Mode" (a pet name for Brie's uninhibited alter-ego), fancy tea time with Paige, and Natalya's... bathroom problem.

Total Divas also offered plenty of moving moments. Alexa Bliss shared her experience of suffering from an eating disorder as a teenager. Nia Jax got emotional on a shopping trip with the Bella Twins and admitted to feeling vulnerable about her size. Nikki talked about the career-crushing injuries she had to recover from, while Natalya eulogized her father, WWE Hall of Famer Jim "The Anvil" Neidhart. The popular program has run for nine seasons, and with Ronda Rousey in the cast, it's sure to heat up some more.

Natalya, Nikki Bella, Eva Marie, Brie Bella and Cameron at Brie's bachelorette party in Cabo, Mexico February 19, 2014 .

The cast of *Total Divas* visits the Eiffel Tower in Paris, France October 8, 2015.

Daniel Bryan and Brie Bella at Natalya's wedding June 27, 2013.

71

High-flying Naomi downs Alexa Bliss to win the *SmackDown* Women's Title at *Elimination Chamber 2017*.

Naomi debuted on *RAW* in January 2012 when she danced into the ring with Cameron as part of Brodus Clay's entourage, the Funkadactyls. After suffering a brutal attack by rival tag team the Bella Twins, the Funkadactyls struck back—sparking a deep-seated rivalry. Naomi joined forces with sometime-ally Tamina and NXT newbie Sasha Banks. The trio called themselves Team B.A.D. and battled Team PCB, among others, before disbanding a year later.

After a hiatus from the ring, Naomi debuted on *SmackDown* in 2016, where she set her sights on the *SmackDown* Women's Championship, held then by Alexa Bliss. Naomi was awarded a chance at the title during a bout at the *2017 Elimination Chamber* pay-per-view. In the supercharged battle, it seemed that Bliss would win when she climbed to the top rope and launched at Naomi. But Naomi managed to get her knees up, knocking the wind out of Bliss. One Springboard maneuver later, Naomi had defeated Bliss to become the first African American Superstar to win the *SmackDown* Women's Championship. She won the title again at *WrestleMania 33*, this time in a Six-Pack Challenge Match. Naomi made history again at *WrestleMania 34* when she won the first Women's Battle Royal, besting a ring full of Superstars including Becky Lynch, Peyton Royce, Sasha Banks, and Bayley.

NAOMI

This driven Superstar's personality blazes as brightly as her eye-catching ring gear. Whether she's part of a tag team or battling solo, Naomi is a history-making competitor whose energetic matches shouldn't be missed!

"I'm here to glow. And my glow will always be on."

—NAOMI

"A good champion accepts and loves competition. I think the more women I face, the more experience I have in the ring, it's only going to make me a better performer."

—NAOMI

DANCING IN AND OUT OF THE RING

A former professional dancer, Naomi brings that coordination, grace, and precision to her matches. She started dancing when she was eight years old, with the goal of attending a dance school. She tried out as a dancer for the Orlando Magic NBA dance team and won a spot. Even before she sashayed onto RAW and SmackDown, she turned heads in NXT. On the first all-women season of NXT, Naomi paired up with Kelly Kelly. She danced circles around the competition, until Kaitlyn bested her in the final week of the season.

All smiles—Naomi and best buddy Kelly Kelly enter the arena: NXT, Nov. 23, 2010.

73

THE NXT SUPERSTARS

If the women who started the Revolution have one thing in common, it's their time in sports entertainment's toughest training ground: NXT.

Paige screams as Emma presses a knee into her back on NXT, February 27, 2014.

Stephanie McMahon may have announced the Revolution in WWE's women's division on *RAW*, stating female Superstars would be given more opportunities under the red brand, but NXT was where the match was lit, the flames were fanned, and the fire was started.

NXT, while a popular brand in its own right, is a springboard for the next generation of *RAW* and *SmackDown* Superstars. Those who feature on the show often go on to compete in the two flagship brands.

From NXT's inception, the program started churning out amazing moments featuring women in the ring. It was the result of a perfect storm of opportunity: NXT gave women highlighted matches as well as time to fully showcase their talent and skills.

While the female Superstars of *RAW* and *SmackDown* still competed for the Divas Championship, the NXT title was called the NXT Women's Championship. Then-up-and-coming NXT stars such as Paige and Becky

Lynch were coached by Sarah Amato, WWE's first-ever female trainer and a successful women's sports entertainer herself. NXT also featured WWE's first full-time female referee, Jessika Carr, who is also a trained sports entertainment star.

The amazing rivalries NXT nurtured, such as that between Asuka and Ember Moon and between Bayley and Sasha Banks, demonstrated that women Superstars could pull just as much—if not more—fan fervour as the men, if given equal opportunity.

Jessika Carr, WWE's first female referee, calls the shots in the ring on NXT, April 10, 2019.

Ember Moon and Asuka launch at each other with high-flying kicks, April 1, 2017.

WWE's first-ever female trainer Sarah Amato working with Paige, March 4, 2014.

Sasha Banks twists Bayley into a painful Bank Statement, October 7, 2015.

WRESTLEMANIA 30

THE VICKIE GUERRERO DIVAS CHAMPIONSHIP INVITATIONAL MATCH

AJ Lee defended her title against the entire women's roster, which meant taking on 13 of the most athletic Superstars in WWE.

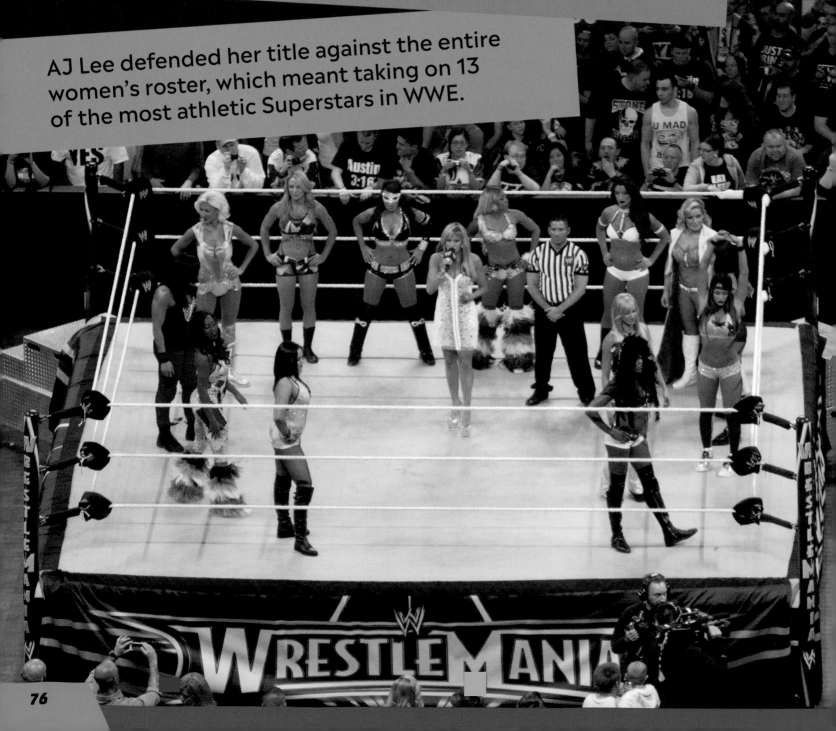

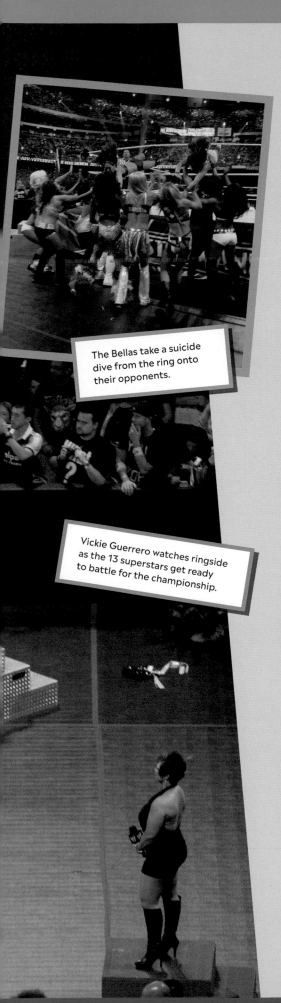

The Bellas take a suicide dive from the ring onto their opponents.

Vickie Guerrero watches ringside as the 13 superstars get ready to battle for the championship.

The Vickie Guerrero Divas Championship Invitational was announced on the March 24, 2014, episode of *RAW*. At the time, Divas Champion AJ Lee was in the middle of a record-breaking reign. At the Invitational, AJ was to defend her title against the entire 13-Divas roster—at the same time! To prove her domination of the division, she would need to overcome Natalya, Naomi, Cameron, Eva Marie, Summer Rae, Nikki Bella, Brie Bella, Aksana, Layla, Emma, Alicia Fox, Rosa Mendes, and AJ's own friend Tamina Snuka. The first Superstar—any Superstar— to score a pinfall or submission would be the winner and new Divas Champion. So, AJ Lee could lose her title even if she wasn't the one pinned. The match was the first and only time the Divas Championship was defended in *WrestleMania*.

EXCUSE ME!

The match started with a Vickie Guerrero cackle and the ring of the bell. The Divas immediately kicked AJ and Tamina to the center of the mat, huddled up, and attacked. From the first moments, it was clear that the match would be chaos. In the fracas, it was hard to see how the referee could even tell what was happening. Natalya tried a triple Sharpshooter on Alicia, Rosa, and Cameron, but Eva Marie swept in and tried to pin her. Natalya broke out.

When four Divas executed simultaneous suplexes and covers, the referee started counting—for anyone! Somehow, everyone broke out of their pin at the same time. Summer Rae took aim at the Divas Champion, but AJ quickly countered, slamming her into the turnbuckle. As AJ turned around, Cameron gave her a big boot out of the ring. The action continued: Emma sandwiched

Summer Rae, Alicia chopped down Emma, Layla knocked out Alicia, Aksana bodyslammed Layla, Natalya clotheslined Aksana, Rosa took care of Natalya, and Eva Marie made the mistake of stepping up to Tamina.

FAIR GAME?

At one point, The Bellas were left alone in the ring. Instead of attacking each other, they simultaneously took a suicide dive to knock down the other Divas. Alone in the ring once more, the sisters finally turned on each other. Nikki gave Brie one Bella of a backbreaker. She was one count away from the win when Natalya and Alicia interrupted. The ring continued to churn with brawling Superstars, until AJ Lee wrapped Naomi up in a Black Widow submission move. The ref called the match, thinking that Naomi had tapped out. But it was a little sleight of hand; AJ was secretly moving her arm.

By skill and some sleight of hand, AJ Lee fends off the entire Divas roster to retain her championship.

Paige becomes the first-ever NXT Women's Champion, June 20, 2013.

Born to pro-wrestling parents, Paige grew up in Norwich, England, and began her career in sports entertainment at the ripe old age of 13. After training in Europe, she moved to the US in 2012 to try her luck in WWE's NXT division. As it turned out, she took the division by storm. Battling Superstars such as Sasha Banks and Emma, Paige quickly shook things up by going on an incredible undefeated streak that ended only when Summer Rae took advantage of Paige's badly injured shoulder in Rae's debut NXT match on February 13, 2013.

That same year, Stephanie McMahon announced that NXT would, for the first time ever, have its own Women's Championship. The winner would be determined by a tournament. Paige defeated Tamina, Alicia Fox, and finally Emma for the honor of being the inaugural female NXT Women's Champion. Paige had reigned over NXT for 274 days when she showed up on *RAW* in April 2014. Intending to congratulate her former NXT competitor AJ Lee on her recent Divas Title win, Paige instead got roped into a spur-of-the-moment Championship Match called by AJ. Paige withstood AJ's Black Widow move and pinned her to become the new Divas Champion. In doing so, she became the youngest Divas Title winner ever at 21, the only woman to hold both the NXT Women's Championship and the Divas Championship, and the first Diva to win a title in a debut match. Needless to say, Paige didn't just set the bar for the women's division at that moment—she snapped that bar in half.

PAIGE
"THE ANTI-DIVA"

This fierce Goth broke the mold in more ways than one in the women's division. From her dark style to her potent grappling skills and striking ring presence, she fanned the flames of the revolution among women Superstars.

Paige was a tireless supporter of new talent and campaigned for pulling NXT newcomers up to the mainstage. A key part of the Divas Revolution, Paige joined Charlotte and Becky Lynch to form Team PCB. Together, they would take on the other triple tag teams in the women's division: Team B.A.D.—Naomi, Sasha Banks, and Tamina; and Team Bella—Nikki and Brie Bella and Alicia Fox. Paige led Team PCB to victories at *Battleground* and *SummerSlam*. She later formed Absolution with NXT alumnae Mandy Rose and Sonya Deville. Paige announced her retirement due to neck injuries in a tearful goodbye the day after *WrestleMania 34* as the WWE Universe chanted, "This is your house!"

> "I just came to do what no one else would."
>
> —PAIGE

Paige calls the shots in her new role as *SmackDown* GM, *SmackDown*, July 24, 2018.

GOODBYES AREN'T FOREVER

No longer able to compete in the ring, Paige still managed to shake things up in WWE. On April 10, 2018, the day after she retired, Shane McMahon announced that Daniel Bryan would be stepping down as *SmackDown* General Manager. His successor would be—Paige. Her first order of business as GM was hugely popular: Daniel Bryan versus the reigning WWE Champion, AJ Styles. Paige left the role in late 2018, and began managing the Kabuki Warriors tag team, featuring Asuka and Kairi Sane.

A women's *RAW* tag team match that was over in almost the blink of an eye spurred the WWE Universe to action.

On the February 23, 2015, episode of *RAW*, Paige and Emma were slated for a tag team match with The Bella Twins. The four Superstars were scuffling before the match even started, and Emma had to hold Paige back from attacking! When the bell rang, Emma and Brie entered the ring first while Paige screamed at Nikki from the ropes, "You're a cheater, Nikki!"

Brie knocked Paige off the side of the ring, then turned her attention to Emma. All it took was Brie delivering a jumping facebuster and one, two, three—the Bellas had won.

Not wanting to accept defeat, Paige leaped into the ring and kicked Brie before Nikki retaliated. And that was it. It was the only Divas match on the entire show, and it was a short one.

The WWE Universe took to social media. Instantly, the hashtag #GiveDivasAChance began trending on Twitter. Fans said the women deserved longer matches. They talked about how the women we just as important as the men. They praised their hard work, hard knocks, and dedication.

Some Superstars even weighed in. Mick Foley tweeted, "I have long been a #DivasBeliever." AJ Lee also chimed in, saying that the women Superstars pulled in merchandising dollars and ratings. The voice of the WWE Universe couldn't be denied. Mr. McMahon responded: "We hear you. Keep watching."

The Bellas, the reigning "Divas of WWE," stride to the ring ready for battle.

Brie Bella connects with a powerful big boot to Emma's midsection.

Paige refuses to lose without a fight and kicks Brie Bella after the bell.

Nikki Bella stands victorious after reminding Paige and Emma who the Divas Champion is.

THE REVOLUTION HAS

NXT SUPERSTARS DEBUT VS. TEAM BELLA, RAW: JULY 13, 2015

Team Bella are none too pleased to receive a talking-to from Stephanie McMahon.

The Bella Twins reigned over the entire women's division in 2015. Nikki Bella, who had been the Divas Champion for more than a year, saying as much in a speech on *RAW*, boasting "I am the Total Diva." During her 232-day reign, Nikki claimed she'd given every woman Superstar a shot at her title, and none could beat her.

The twins had joined with Alicia Fox to form "Team Bella," and they were unstoppable, fending off weeks of challenges by Paige, Tamina, and Naomi. "We are dominant," Nikki declared. "Us three make the decisions in this division. We run it; we rule it."

Of course, Stephanie McMahon didn't take kindly to that kind of talk. Since #GiveDivasAChance had trended worldwide on Twitter, Stephanie had taken an active interest in the women's division She strode to the ring to set Team Bella straight. "Let me be very clear: I own WWE," Stephanie said. She had been thinking about WWE's legacy and the revolution happening in women's sports in general. "Women are making their mark," she said. And Stephanie made it clear that she intended to answer the WWE Universe's call for a bigger spotlight on female Superstars. Stephanie called Paige to the ring and credited her as the woman who had the courage to try to shake things up in WWE. To make change happen, however, Stephanie said Paige would need more than courage alone. She then announced that Paige would have backup. Stephanie called in NXT Superstars Becky Lynch and Charlotte Flair to help Paige even the score against Team Bella.

Then Naomi and Tamina arrived. "We got some unfinished business with the Bellas *and* with Paige," Naomi told Stephanie. "We're all the competition you need." To even out the teams, Stephanie added Sasha Banks to Naomi and Tamina's team. To this, the WWE Universe erupted in chants of "This is awesome!" And the members of the refreshed Divas division erupted in battle in the ring as Stephanie looked on, smiling. The women who had revolutionized NXT had arrived on *RAW*.

BEGUN

"**Things are going to change— starting right now.**"
—STEPHANIE MCMAHON

Tensions begin to rise as Charlotte Flair enters the ring and the Superstars face off.

The new Divas immediately clash with the new arrivals from NXT in a high-energy brawl.

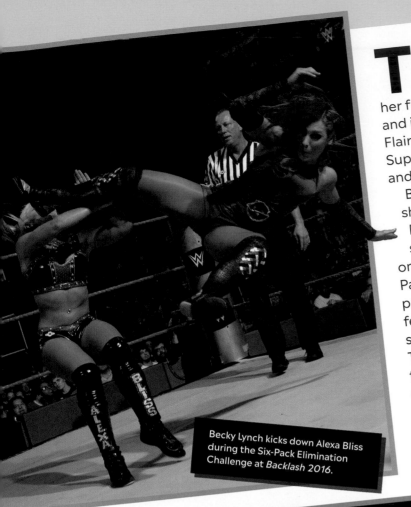

To become "The Man," Becky had to systematically work her way through the women's division. After training in Ireland and England, and facing off against her future rivals in NXT, Becky joined *RAW*'s roster in 2015, and immediately formed in alliance with Paige and Charlotte Flair to create Team PCB. She took on the top female Superstars of the day, such as Naomi and Sasha Banks, and even defeated Brie Bella at *WWE Main Event* that year. Becky was the most valuable player of PCB when she pinned Brie Bella to win the Divas Triple Tag Team Elimination Match at *SummerSlam 2015*. But then the stable turned on each other, and Becky found herself on the receiving end of attacks from her former teammates, Paige and Charlotte. A rocky road was ahead as Becky pursued the WWE Women's Championship but regularly fell short of the title. Her fortunes began to change when she was the first woman drafted to *SmackDown* in 2016. The *SmackDown* Women's Championship was introduced the same year, and Becky became the first titleholder when she defeated Natalya, Naomi, Alexa Bliss, Carmella, and Nikki Bella in a Six-Pack Elimination Challenge at *Backlash* 2016. Alexa Bliss would take the title from Becky in a Tables Match at *TLC 2016*, after which Becky had two long, unsuccessful years.

Becky Lynch kicks down Alexa Bliss during the Six-Pack Elimination Challenge at *Backlash 2016*.

BECKY LYNCH
"THE MAN"

"Straight Fire," "The Irish Lass Kicker," and "Becky Balboa"; Becky Lynch goes by many names, but one that sums her up better than any other: The Man.

> "I hope the other WWE Superstars, regardless of gender, are paying attention to the attitude of Becky Lynch."
>
> —JOHN CENA

> ## "From now on, I'm getting what I deserve."
> —BECKY LYNCH

In 2018, Lynch battled her way to a winning streak and an eventual title win against Charlotte Flair at *Hell in a Cell*. Once again, as *SmackDown*'s top female Superstar, Becky decided she was WWE's top dog and began calling herself "The Man." She also decided to take matters into her own hands—and take over WWE. Attacking Ronda Rousey backstage with a Dis-Arm-Her maneuver, Becky lead the *SmackDown* Superstars to invade *RAW* during the November 12 episode and a vicious brawl ensued. She eventually lost her title to Asuka, but a *Royal Rumble* win would put Becky on track to challenge and defeat both Ronda and Charlotte Flair at *WrestleMania* 35 for the *RAW* Women's Championship and the *SmackDown* Championship. Becky fought her way to the top of the women's division—and pushed the bar even higher when The Man became known as "Becky Two Belts": the first woman ever to hold the *RAW* and *SmackDown* Women's Titles at the same time.

"Becky Two Belts" shows off the *RAW* and *SmackDown* Women's titles, at *WrestleMania* 35.

Charlotte's first championship win was in May 2014. To earn it, she worked through an eight-woman tournament to face off against Natalya at *NXT TakeOver* (with Ric Flair and Bret Hart in attendance). Charlotte reigned for 258 days, regularly tangling with Superstars such as Becky Lynch, Sasha Banks, and Bayley.

When she arrived on *RAW* in July 2015, Charlotte kept working and winning. She formed Team PCB with Paige and Becky Lynch. She kicked off a pay-per-view winning streak at *Battleground* the same year that she defeated Sasha and Brie Bella in a Triple Threat Match. And in the first-ever Divas Beat the Clock Challenge, Charlotte quickly beat Brie with one minute and 40 seconds left on the clock to win her chance at Nikki Bella's Divas Title—which Charlotte got at *Night of Champions 2015*.

Though her Divas Title victory broke up Team PCB—Paige turned on Charlotte, and Charlotte eventually turned on Becky—Charlotte could rule just fine on her own. At *WrestleMania 32*, when the WWE Women's Championship replaced the Divas Championship, Charlotte was—of course—the first Superstar to hold the title by defeating Sasha and Becky in a Triple Threat Match. She reigned for 113 days.

The *RAW* Women's Championship was established in August 2016, and Charlotte won it, retaining it in the *Clash of Champions*. When she moved to *SmackDown* in 2017, Charlotte eventually bested Natalya to gain that women's title too. In March 2019, Charlotte defeated Asuka to win the *SmackDown* Women's Championship again—and with it, she broke the record for number of women's titles held, at eight. (Trish Stratus previously held the record with seven title wins.) Charlotte is also the first Superstar to hold the NXT, Divas, *RAW*, and *SmackDown* Women's Championships, and she participated in the first-ever women's main event at *WrestleMania 35*. Charlotte is true sports entertainment royalty.

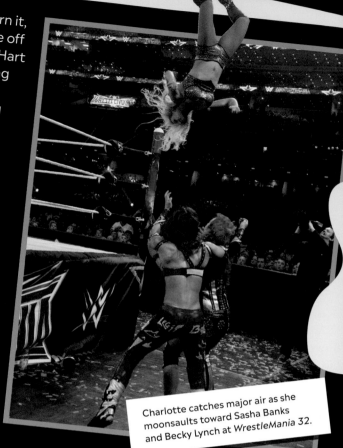

Charlotte catches major air as she moonsaults toward Sasha Banks and Becky Lynch at *WrestleMania* 32.

CHARLOTTE FLAIR
"GENETICALLY SUPERIOR"

Whether she's breaking records, holding winning streaks, or collecting championships, there's no doubt about it: Charlotte just plain rules.

> **" I fear nothing, and a true champion fears no one. "**
>
> —CHARLOTTE

Beaming, WWE Legend Ric Flair celebrates his daughter's SmackDown Women's Championship win, Starrcade, November 25, 2017.

THE APPLE DOESN'T FALL FAR

As the daughter of WWE Legend Nature Boy Ric Flair, Charlotte's sports entertainment success might seem like "natural selection." Charlotte's certainly not one to disagree. She regularly brags that she's a "genetically superior athlete." Charlotte's father is often ringside to support her—and sometimes even interfere a little bit. Though the two had a dramatic dispute in 2016, they mended their relationship. After all, the family that shouts "WOOOOO!" together, stays together.

GENERATIONS

It took determination, dedication, skill, and training for each female Superstar to enter sports entertainment. But in some cases, the inspiration came from a family member who was also sports entertainment royalty.

NIA JAX

Sports entertainment has deep roots in Nia Jax's family. Her cousin is The Rock, who hails from the Maivia family; her uncle, High Chief Peter Maivia, was a sports entertainment Superstar; and his wife, Lia, was a promoter. Nia had designs on becoming a WNBA basketball star, but attending 2012's *WrestleMania XXVIII* alongside her aunt (The Rock's mom) inspired her to follow in her family's footsteps and take her talents to the mat. An unstoppable mix of beauty and brawn, "The Irresistible Force" is an inspiration to WWE fans everywhere.

> **"I thought it was one of the coolest things I'd ever seen."**
>
> —NIA JAX, ON SEEING HIGH CHIEF PETER MAIVIA WITH A CHAMPIONSHIP BELT

High Chief Peter Maivia challenges WWE Champion Bob Backlund, c. 1978.

Jim Neidhart taunts his opponent with a his trademark laugh, c. 1991.

Ric Flair traps Bret Hart in a hammerlock, c. 1991.

CHARLOTTE FLAIR

With her "Wooooo!" war cry, Figure Eight Leglock, and bedazzled garb, Charlotte Flair honors her dad's style. Her theme music is even a club remix of his entrance song. Her dad just might be her biggest fan. "Nature Boy" Ric Flair was a 16-time WWE Champion of skill and swagger. Whether fans remember him from his time with The Four Horsemen faction or for his fancy robes, he's left an indelible imprint on WWE. Ric is tremendously proud of Charlotte's achievements. He tries to be at all of her biggest matches, and has a habit of getting teary whenever he's in the ring with her.

> ❝She's not Ric Flair's daughter. I'm Charlotte Flair's dad.❞
>
> —RIC FLAIR

NATALYA

When people say sports entertainment runs in the blood, it's especially true of Natalya. Her grandfather is Hall of Famer Stu Hart. Her uncle is Bret "Hit Man" Hart. And her father was Jim "The Anvil" Neidhart. A gifted shotputter and football player, he was a powerhouse who reportedly got his nickname from an actual anvil-throwing contest. Natalya is as proud as can be of her family legacy, and she's always carrying the Hart Family torch. Her former team, the "Hart Dynasty," her punishing Sharpshooter move, and the pink in her ring outfits are a nod to those who came before her. When Jim Neidhart passed away during the week leading up to *SummerSlam 2018*, Natalya decided to participate in his honor. She wore her dad's jacket down the ramp to the ring.

> ❝I'm not saying goodbye to my dad, I've decided. I just have an extra angel in heaven.❞
>
> — NATALYA

Hailing from Boston (or "Bosstown"), Sasha Banks got her start in WWE by taking NXT by storm. Sasha won her first NXT Women's Championship by defeating Charlotte Flair in a Fatal 4-Way on NXT on February 11, 2015. Though she lost the title to Bayley in *NXT TakeOver: Brooklyn* in 2015, she did it in one of the most spectacular matches in women's sports entertainment history.

Sasha's time in *RAW* was no less amazing. She debuted on the July 13, 2015, episode alongside Charlotte Flair and Becky Lynch. Stephanie McMahon brought in "The Boss" to ally with Naomi and Tamina, and together the three formed Team B.A.D. (Beautiful and Dangerous). A year later, she took the WWE Women's Championship from Charlotte to begin the first of her four reigns.

If there was a next step that the women's division hadn't taken yet, Sasha was there to march ahead. She competed in the first-ever women's Iron Man Match, Hell in a Cell Match, pay-per-view main event match, match in the Middle East, Royal Rumble Match, Elimination Chamber Match, and the first Women's Tag Team Title Match. Whether Sasha's talking smack on the microphone, paving the way for new, more challenging women's matches, or ruthlessly turning on a former friend, you can always expect "The Legit Boss" of sports entertainment to make a statement.

SASHA BANKS
"THE LEGIT BOSS"

Instantly recognizable from her confident swagger and trademark brightly colored hair, Sasha Banks has taken part in some of the biggest moments in WWE's women's division.

> "You don't need luck when you're The Boss."
>
> —SASHA BANKS

Sasha strides to the ring alongside Tamina and Naomi, also known as Team B.A.D on SmackDown, September 29, 2015.

TAG IN THE BOSS

Given her ego and excellent solo game, it may come as a surprise to some that The Boss is also a gifted tag team competitor. She formed BFFs—Beautiful, Fierce Females —with Summer Rae in NXT. The team had an undefeated streak before it dissolved so the women could pursue the NXT Women's Championship separately. Sasha also teamed with Becky Lynch in the short-lived Team B.A.E. (Best at Everything). In RAW, Sasha and Team B.A.D., in various configurations, worked through the women's roster until Sasha decided to strike out on her own in 2016. After a budding rivalry—and ensuing counseling—she and on-again, off-again ally Bayley formed the Boss 'n' Hug Connection, rising to the top of women's tag team competition. Even with her successful stables, it's clear that The Boss—and only The Boss—is priority #1. Beware!

Team Bella: Alicia Fox, Nikki Bella, and Brie Bella are confident they are the dominant force in the Divas division.

Not about to let Team Bella run the Divas division, Team B.A.D.—Tamina, Naomi, and Sasha Banks—get ready to rough things up.

A TRIPLE TAG TEAM

TEAM BELLA BATTLE TEAM PCB AND TEAM B.A.D.

When Stephanie introduced newcomers Sasha Banks, Becky Lynch, and Charlotte Flair on the July 13, 2015, episode of *RAW*, a battle immediately broke out: the Divas Revolution had started with a bang. With the lines drawn, Team PCB (Paige, Charlotte, Becky), Team B.A.D. (Tamina, Sasha, Naomi), and Team Bella (Nikki and Brie Bella, Alicia Fox) were keen to transform the women's competition. Each team was in a race to prove they were the supreme athletes in the division.

The newcomers made their mark quickly, with PCB scoring a big first victory when Charlotte pinned Nikki in a tag team matchup on *RAW*. Sasha also came out on top during her first match with Nikki.

Just one month after forming, PCB and Team B.A.D. met Team Bella at *SummerSlam 2015* in a three-team Elimination Match. Per match rules, all it would take was for one Superstar in a tag team to be pinned

or submit for the entire team to be eliminated.

Team B.A.D. had quick tags at the beginning of the match, keeping Becky busy and sequestered in their corner. When Tamina took Becky out of the ring and Charlotte intervened, Sasha and Naomi went airborne over the top rope to join the fray, followed quickly by soaring Bella Twins and a high-flying Paige.

YOU WIN SOME, YOU LOSE SOME

Back in the ring, Team Bella dominated and eliminated Team B.A.D. The match almost looked over when Nikki hit Becky with a big Rack Attack, but Paige pulverized her. Then Nikki got Paige outside the ring and nearly broke her with a painful Alabama Slam. Beating a countout, Paige dragged herself back into the ring for more punishment. In a quick turnaround, Paige caught Alicia Fox with a big knee, and Charlotte tagged in with chops and a spear. Nikki

Team Bella, Team PCB, and Team B.A.D. prepare for a showdown, Battleground July 19, 2015.

RIVALRY

floored Charlotte with a punch to the gut. Becky finally tagged in and landed a pump handle move to flip Brie for the win.

PCB's victory was short-lived: Team Bella won their next face-off with PCB on *RAW*. Though PCB worked well together, they were no match for the Bellas' twin strategies of distraction and interference.

When Paige and Becky took on Naomi and Sasha Banks, Team B.A.D. also bested PCB with their trademark fast tags to maximize punishment. This time, it was Becky who took a beating. Paige was able to tag in, finally, but Naomi flipped her for the pin.

DIVISIONS ARISE

By late September 2015, Charlotte had forced Nikki to tap out and hand over her Divas Championship at *Night of Champions*. But Charlotte's hard-fought win spelled disaster for PCB. Paige turned on her former friend over the title. When a Miz TV moment transformed into an impromptu six-Diva tag team match with Team Bella vs. Team PCB. PCB initially showed a unified front against their common enemies, but after being accidentally bumped by Charlotte, Paige left the ring in a huff. Natalya tried to intervene, but Paige attacked her. Distracted, Charlotte fell to Nikki's Rack Attack.

As Team PCB began to implode, Team B.A.D. were showing Team Bella who was boss, with Sasha forcing Alicia Fox to tap out of a Bank Statement. Despite showing promise, B.A.D. eventually disintegrated, too, when Sasha decided to fly solo after the Divas Championship.

PCB and B.A.D. were two of the most dynamic teams in the women's division, but in the end, when it came down to their individual members, it was every Superstar for herself. What worked for Team Bella was loyalty.

A BRAND-NEW TITLE

WRESTLEMANIA 32: THE DIVAS CHAMPIONSHIP IS RETIRED

> **"May the best woman win."**
>
> —LITA

Team Total Divas celebrate their victory over Team B.A.D. & Blonde.

During the *WrestleMania 32* Kickoff Show, Team Total Divas (Paige, Eva Maria, Brie Bella, Natalya, Alicia Fox) took on Team B.A.D. & Blonde (Lana, Tamina, Emma, Naomi, Summer Rae) in a raucous Ten-Woman Tag Team Match. With as much drama between the Total Divas team members as between the teams, Team B.A.D. & Blonde had the upperhand through most of the match. Paige weathered beatings from Emma, Lana, Tamina, and Naomi before digging deep and catching all of the B.A.D. & Blondes outside the ring in a flying crossbody move. After quick tags—which made it hard to tell who the legal women in the ring should be—Brie Bella nabbed the victory for Total Divas by making Naomi submit to a "Yes!" lock. Team Total Divas were joined in their celebration by Nikki Bella, who was wearing a brace as she recuperated from neck surgery.

And that wasn't even the most exciting event in the show. With 30 minutes left to the beginning of the "Show of all Shows," Lita took to the ring for an announcement. She talked about how she remembered *WrestleMania I*, when Cyndi Lauper raised Wendi Richter's hand. Lita said she knew then that she wanted to be on the "Grandest Stage of Them All." Speaking of The Fabulous Moolah, Mae Young, Sensational Sherri, Alundra Blayze, Jacqueline, and Trish Stratus, Lita said, "It was these women that paved the way for a whole new division." Later that evening, during *WrestleMania 32*, Charlotte Flair, Becky Lynch, and Sasha Banks were scheduled for a Triple Threat Match for the Divas Title. Instead, Lita said, the Divas Championship would be retired. "They are so much more than "Divas" in this ring today. They are all WWE Superstars." And with that, she unveiled the WWE Women's Championship.

Alicia Fox goes airborne to connect hit Emma with a powerful kick.

The referee steps in as Team Total Divas clash with the B.A.D. & Blonde.

Brie Bella lifts Naomi up before slamming her down into the mat.

Bayley has worked her way from underdog to top dog one Bayley-to-Belly suplex at a time. Her WWE career began when she joined NXT in 2012. She cut her teeth in her trademark big grin battling NXT stars such as Paige, Emma, and Alicia Fox. When Bayley squared off for a title shot with NXT Women's Champion Sasha Banks, aka "The Boss," at *NXT TakeOver: Brooklyn*, she was the clear underdog—and fan favorite. The energetic bout is considered one of the best women's matches of all time. By the time it was over, Bayley had proven her in-ring skills and was the new NXT Women's Champion.

Bayley and Sasha met again at NXT *TakeOver: Respect* in the first-ever 30-minute Women's Iron Man Match. A true test of endurance, Bayley just eked out a 3–2 victory to retain her NXT Women's Title.

Bayley reigned as champ for 223 days, until Asuka ended her streak at *NXT TakeOver: Dallas*. *RAW* General Manager Mick Foley brought Bayley to the red brand, where she rejoined many of her former NXT competitors. After a long rivalry with Charlotte Flair's protégée Dana Brooke, Bayley took on Charlotte herself, and won the *RAW* Women's Title. Bayley also teamed up with Sasha Banks to become Women's Tag Team Champions.

The championships kept coming. After Bayley moved from *RAW* to *SmackDown* during the 2019 Superstar Shakeup, she won the Women's Money in the Bank Ladder Match, toppling six other competitors—most notably, devious Superstars Sonya Deville and Mandy Rose—to win the contract. She cashed it in that night, defeating Charlotte Flair to become *SmackDown* Women's Champion.

BAYLEY

Once the smiley face of WWE, when Bayley joined *SmackDown* in 2019, she decided to do away with hugs and unleash the strong, win-at-any-costs athlete within.

> **"Right now you're probably realizing DAMN, Bayley's good and the whole world gets to see it."**
>
> —BAYLEY

Alexa Bliss is on the receiving end of a double-dropkick from Sasha and Bayley on *RAW*, February 26, 2018.

FRIENDS FOREVER?

Bayley and Sasha Banks have one of the most complicated relationships in sports entertainment. Sasha was Bayley's first opponent in WWE, but since then they've battled each other in memorable matches, teamed up, and turned on each other when it counted the most. After Sasha eliminated Bayley in the first-ever Women's Royal Rumble Match and kicked her down in the first-ever Women's Elimination Chamber Match, even Bayley couldn't take it anymore. She leaped away from Sasha's tag during a tag team match. Eventually, Bayley and The Boss went to counseling together, and the result was the Boss 'n' Hug Connection: a lovable, but badass tag team.

A GAME-CHANGING

NXT TAKEOVER: BROOKLYN, AUGUST 22, 2015

Bayley got her shot at Sasha Banks's NXT Women's Championship in a battle that became an instant classic.

Announcing the NXT Women's Title Match in Brooklyn that night, Stephanie McMahon talked about the Divas Revolution that she'd set in motion a month earlier in *RAW*. "Make no mistake about it," she said, "that Revolution started right here in NXT with some extraordinary women."

Bayley, finally healed from a hand injury, was ready. She'd missed a lot of opportunities while she was out, but now she was back and had worked her way to a title bout with "The Boss," Sasha Banks, who had recently joined Team B.A.D. on *RAW*. Sasha, who had reigned for 192 days, wasn't about to let the underdog get the upper hand.

Before the match begins, Sasha Banks lets Bayley know exactly who's "The Boss."

GIVE UP!

Sasha immediately tried to get in Bayley's head, mercilessly taunting her. But her words made Bayley spring into action, and the two Superstars traded vicious blows. When Sasha kicked Bayley's legs out from under her as she stood on the ropes, Bayley fell to the floor, faceplanting on the edge of the ring on her way down.

Back in the ring, Sasha worked on Bayley's neck and then wrapped her in a straitjacket hold, screaming "Give up, Bayley!" Sasha talked smack, grinning so much it looked like she was enjoying it. Sasha strung Bayley up in the ring corner, climbed to the top rope and then dropped, kneeing Bayley in the midsection. Outside the ring, as Bayley writhed, "The Boss" ripped off Bayley's arm brace and began, cruelly, to work her hand. Sasha slid Bayley's hand between the LED board and the steel steps and kicked. As the ref leaned over to check on Bayley, Sasha even swan-dived over him to attack her.

Back in the ring, it seemed like that had to be it for Bayley. Sasha attempted a pin, but Bayley still kicked out. A look of frustration crossed Sasha's face.

Sasha grins as she pushes down on Bayley in an attempt to weaken her.

Sasha does her best to fight off Bayley's attack from the ropes.

MAIN EVENT

THE UNDERDOG BITES BACK

Bayley attacked with double ax handle punches, cradling her hurt hand in the other. She then issued a big suplex to Sasha in the ring corner, but "The Boss" wouldn't quit. She smashed Bayley's face into the mat and then went into a Bank Statement move. As Bayley strained for the rope to break the submission hold, Sasha ferociously stomped on her injured hand. Somehow, Bayley touched the rope and reversed the hold, wrapping Sasha up in her own Bank Statement.

After a Bayley-to-Belly Suplex, Sasha still kicked out. Bayley repeatedly tried to get the stunned Sasha into a big move from the top rope, but Sasha fought back, pushing her down again and again. Finally, Sasha gathered all of her energy and took a big leap from the top rope, landing on Bayley. With Bayley's arms and legs pinned, Sasha's victory seemed inevitable. Until Bayley broke the cover *again*.

Bayley gets the upper hand and some momentum to slam Sasha to the mat.

Finally, Bayley was able to tangle Sasha up on the top rope and flip her. After that and one big Bayley-to-Belly Suplex, Bayley finally won the match and the title.

The battle was hailed as one of the best matches ever seen, not just in the women's division, but in the whole of sports entertainment, and a key moment in the Women's Evolution.

Bayley digs deep and fights back to win the NXT Women's Championship.

> **"Women's wrestling is back."**
>
> —THE ANNOUNCE TEAM

WOMEN ENTER THE

THE FIRST WOMEN'S HELL IN A CELL MATCH, SASHA BANKS VS. CHARLOTTE FLAIR

Sasha launches off the steel cage onto Charlotte as she lays helpless on the mat.

As the revolution in the women's division gained momentum, the challenges the Superstars faced became increasingly difficult.

Before 2016, not a single woman had competed inside the steel cage in any of WWE's previous 35 Hell in a Cell Matches. This would also be the first time a women's match had ever been the main event at a pay-per-view event. Sasha Banks was set to defend the Women's Championship against Charlotte Flair at *Hell in a Cell*. At the contract signing for the match, *Hell in a Cell* veteran Mick Foley cautioned Sasha and Charlotte about what the steel

cage can do. The "demonic structure," Foley said, was like a third competitor.

A DELAYED START
At the event in the TD Garden in Boston, Charlotte was transported to the ring on a throne carried by her own cadre of gladiators. She was boasting a 13–0 record in solo matches at pay-per-view events and 12–0 at title matches. "The Boss," Sasha Banks, also arrived in style in a Cadillac Escalade with a band of bodyguards, ready to prove herself in her home town.

The action moves to the walls of the cell as Charlotte and Sasha climb the steel cage.

CELL

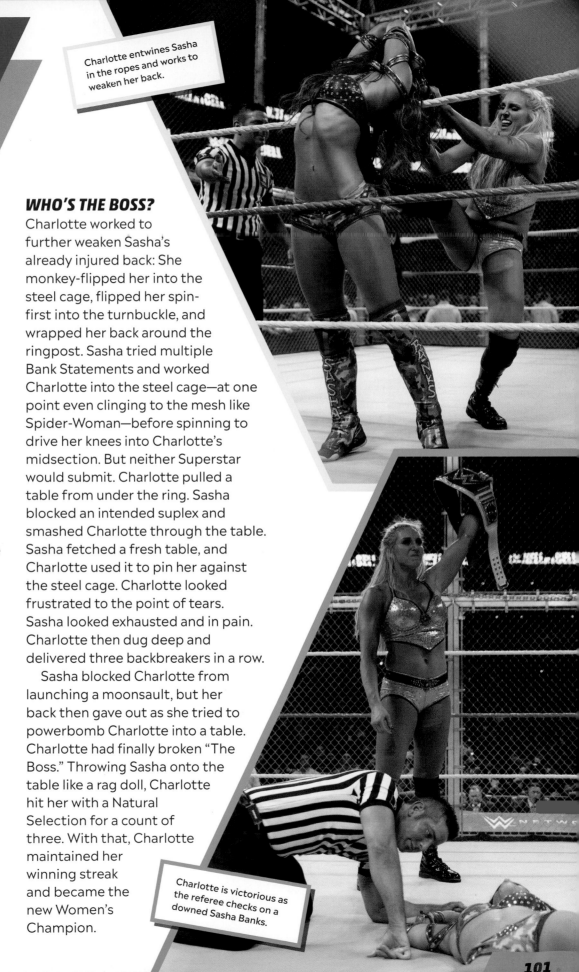

Charlotte entwines Sasha in the ropes and works to weaken her back.

MAKE IT OFFICIAL

As the match was set to begin, both Superstars watched the cage lower from the arena rafters. In a flash, Charlotte blindsided Sasha, throwing her out of the ring and under the descending steel cage. The ref was able to stop the cage to prevent Sasha from being crushed under its weight, but Charlotte leaped from the ropes and battled her in the crowd as the cage finished its descent. The bell still hadn't rung, and the referees tried to usher Charlotte and Sasha into the cage to begin the match. Then Charlotte began to climb the cage, and Sasha followed, tugging at her. Charlotte dropped to the ground. As Sasha started to climb back down, Charlotte grabbed her and powerbombed her through the announce table.

The match had still not started, but already Sasha was struggling to stand. The refs pleaded with her to give up as they called for EMTs. The medical team loaded Sasha on to a stretcher and stabilized her neck with a brace.

As the announcer was about to call the match and crown Charlotte the new Women's Champion by forfeit, "The Boss" surged up and ripped off the brace. She could not let that happen. Sasha stormed into the steel cage and commanded the ref to ring the bell and officially start the match with such ferocity that Charlotte begged to be let out. What followed was a brutal match, unlike any seen before in the women's division.

WHO'S THE BOSS?

Charlotte worked to further weaken Sasha's already injured back: She monkey-flipped her into the steel cage, flipped her spin-first into the turnbuckle, and wrapped her back around the ringpost. Sasha tried multiple Bank Statements and worked Charlotte into the steel cage—at one point even clinging to the mesh like Spider-Woman—before spinning to drive her knees into Charlotte's midsection. But neither Superstar would submit. Charlotte pulled a table from under the ring. Sasha blocked an intended suplex and smashed Charlotte through the table. Sasha fetched a fresh table, and Charlotte used it to pin her against the steel cage. Charlotte looked frustrated to the point of tears. Sasha looked exhausted and in pain. Charlotte then dug deep and delivered three backbreakers in a row.

Sasha blocked Charlotte from launching a moonsault, but her back then gave out as she tried to powerbomb Charlotte into a table. Charlotte had finally broken "The Boss." Throwing Sasha onto the table like a rag doll, Charlotte hit her with a Natural Selection for a count of three. With that, Charlotte maintained her winning streak and became the new Women's Champion.

Charlotte is victorious as the referee checks on a downed Sasha Banks.

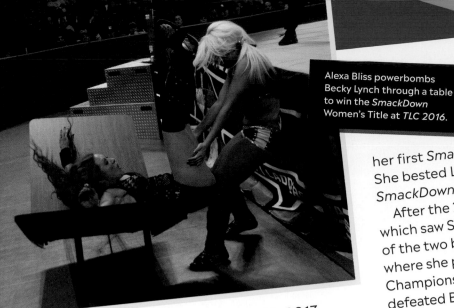

Alexa Bliss debuted in NXT in 2013. As fierce as she was, she had never won the NXT Championship. This was no matter, though, because she was about to take WWE's main brands by storm. Drafted to *SmackDown* in 2016, Alexa quickly got a title opportunity when she faced off against *SmackDown* Women's Champion Becky Lynch in a Tables Match at *TLC*. Though Becky dominated the first half of the match, Alexa was able to take a bite out of the champ (literally). The Superstars exhausted each other until Alexa finally powerbombed Lynch through a table for her first *SmackDown* Women's title. She bested Lynch again for her second *SmackDown* Women's title in 2017.

After the 2017 Superstar Shakeup, which saw Superstars drafted to one of the two brands, Alexa moved to *RAW*, where she pursued the *RAW* Women's Championship. At *Payback 2017*, she defeated Bayley for the title, becoming the first woman ever to have held both the *SmackDown* and the *RAW* title.

In 2018, Alexa became Ms. Money in the Bank after defeating seven other competitors. The second-ever woman to win the MITB contract, Alexa became the first woman to cash it in on the same night. Alexa appeared in the middle of Nia Jax and Ronda Rousey's bout, beat both with the briefcase, and then cashed in to hit a flagging Jax with a Twisted Bliss maneuver to win her third *RAW* Women's title. Alexa may be one of the smaller female Superstars, but nobody can doubt that "The Goddess" is mighty.

ALEXA BLISS
"THE GODDESS OF WWE"

Her name may sound sweet, but Alexa Bliss is a full "Five Feet of Fury." She can go from conducting a lighthearted interview to slamming a rival Superstar through a table in a moment—of Bliss.

"I make history."

—ALEXA BLISS

Alexa Bliss is confident in her role as host of *WrestleMania 35*.

SEVERAL MOMENTS OF BLISS

When Alexa's not wowing in the ring, she hosts her hit talk show segment, "A Moment of Bliss." As the first-ever woman to host a WWE talk show, Alexa asks the tough questions and gets the dirt from her fellow Superstars. Rarely without interruption, "A Moment of Bliss" has seen discussions reach boiling point, challenges issued, and alliances fall apart. Ever the professional, Bliss handles every event like a pro (but keeps herself front and center). Due to her success, Alexa was invited to host "the Grandest Stage of Them All," *WrestleMania 35*.

BEHIND THE MIC

Whether it's interviewing backstage at NXT, firing up crowds of thousands at a WWE pay-per-view event, or tracking the action at the announce table, these women are some of the key voices in sports entertainment.

ALEXA BLISS

The WWE Universe looks forward to the Moment of Bliss segment on *RAW* and Alexa's illuminating interviews with Superstars. Most people think she got the microphone as a result of her Superstar status, but Bliss actually debuted in WWE as a backstage announcer for *NXT Live*.

RENEE YOUNG

Renee Young's first appearance in WWE was March 29, 2012. Since then, she's been back stage and behind the announce table for plenty of WWE events. In September 2018, Young became the first-ever full-time female announcer on *RAW*. This was after she'd already broken the barrier as the first woman to announce a major WWE show in August 2018, when she filled in for Jonathan Coachman on *RAW*.

LILIAN GARCIA

Lilian Garcia debuted as a ring announcer on *RAW Is War* in August 1999. A brilliant singer, she often sang the United States national anthem, "The Star Spangled Banner," for packed audiences before events—most memorably for the first *SmackDown* episode following the September 11 terrorist attacks in New York City. In Garcia's long tenure with the company—she's been with WWE on and off for two decades—she has become the first Latin woman to announce at *WrestleMania*, she announced the first Women's Battle Royal during *WrestleMania 34*'s pre-show and she sang the national anthem at three *WrestleMania*s.

ALICIA TAYLOR

This NXT announcer puts the beat in beatdown. Before joining the NXT announce team to cover Superstars, she was a drummer for pop stars.

CHARLY CARUSO

Backstage announce team member Charly Caruso has one of the toughest jobs in the business: catching amped-up Superstars for interviews behind the scenes. This veteran reporter is quick on her feet and totally unflappable.

2017 MAE YOUNG CLASSIC

As the women's division continues to evolve, the Mae Young Classic gives fans a peek into the future with its awesome roundup of talent.

Rhea Ripley fires up the crowd at the inaugural Mae Young Classic.

Serena Deeb flips Vanessa Borne in an action-packed bout.

Kavita Devi holds Dakota Kai over her head before slamming her to the mat.

Piper Niven attacks Santana Garrett in round one of the tournament.

Xia Li brings her martial arts skills to her match with Mercedes Martinez in round one.

Kairi Sane launches an airborne attack on Shayna Baszler.

> **"The Mae Young Classic was about opportunity and breaking the glass ceiling."**
>
> —TRIPLE H

Named in honor of a sports entertainment veteran and WWE Hall of Famer, the very first Mae Young Classic was announced the weekend of *WrestleMania* 33. Thirty-two women from NXT and independent circuits competed in the tournament, which unfolded over five rounds and aired on August 28, September 4, and September 12, 2017. From the first round of 32, 16 women advanced to the next round, then eight, and so on, until the last two competitors met in the final.

The competition was truly worldwide. The WWE Universe were introduced to stellar athletes from China, India, Japan, New Zealand, Germany, the Dominican Republic, the US, UK, and more.

The women clashed in a mix-up of style, skill, and attitude, and surprises abounded. Athletes who were sports entertainment stars in their home countries sometimes lost to underdogs, as was the case with *luchadora* Princesa Sugehit, who lost to Meredes Martinez. New faces such as Piper Niven came out on top against experienced performers like Serena Deeb. Future NXT Superstars such as Xia Li, Rhea Ripley, and Mia Yim made their WWE debut during the Classic, too.

Shayna Baszler and Kairi Sane (two future NXT Women's Champions) out-battled the 30 other women to meet at the final. In the end, Kairi soared over submission expert Shayna to win the tournament.

Held yearly since the inaugural tournament, the Classic continues to give a boost to exciting new competitors in women's sports entertainment and creates an opportunity for female Superstars to test their mettle on a global scale.

Growing up with her cousin, athlete and WWE Superstar The Rock, it's no real surprise that Nia Jax was a jock when she was a kid. She tried judo, karate, and kickboxing, and played college basketball. In addition to sporting prowess, Nia utilized her strong physique and beauty by working as a model before setting her sights on sports entertainment.

In early 2014, Nia Jax began training at the WWE Performance Center. It quickly became evident that Nia had a power unmatched in WWE's women's division when she crushed the Center's weight lifting records for women. In no time, she was knocking down the women of NXT. In 2015, she squared off against Superstars such as Liv Morgan, Bayley, Carmella, Alexa Bliss, and Asuka. Though she was a force in and out of the ring, she never held the NXT Women's Championship.

On July 19, 2016, Nia was drafted to *RAW*. There, she enjoyed an immediate winning streak and tangled with Alicia Fox and Sasha Banks. She also appeared on the *Total Divas* reality show alongside her bestie, Alexa Bliss. But heartbreak was on the horizon. In 2018, Nia found out Alexa had been using Nia to get her hands on the Women's Championship. Alexa then turned on her friend and insulted Nia, even making fun of her body. "The Irresistible Force" turned pain into payback during *WrestleMania 34*, when she bested her former best friend and walked away with Alexa's *RAW* Women's Title. She lost it again to Alexa at *Money in the Bank* two months later.

Tamina and Nia work together to win the Women's Tag Team Championship Elimination Chamber Qualifying Match against Alexa Bliss and Mickie James, *RAW*, January 28, 2019.

In 2019, Nia teamed up with fellow powerhouse Tamina to make a run for the WWE Women's Tag Team Championship. Though they worked well together, they never succeeded in winning the title. After they battled it out in a fatal 4-way against Sasha Banks and Bayley, The IIconics, and Beth Phoenix and Natalya during *WrestleMania 35*, Nia Jax was diagnosed with injuries in both knees. She had successful surgery in April 2019 and was plotting her return to the ring during rehab. On her return, Nia will continue to inspire the WWE Universe with her body positivity, her dominance, and her winning record.

NIA JAX
"THE IRRESISTIBLE FORCE"

To join WWE, this Superstar turned her back on a successful college basketball career and the glamorous lifestyle of a plus-size model. And lucky for the WWE Universe she did: Nia Jax exhibits an irresistible combination of sheer might and star power in the ring.

"Who wants to be ordinary? Be extraordinary."

—NIA JAX

Nia Jax sneaks up on R-Truth and attacks him before taking his spot in the *Royal Rumble 2019*.

DOUBLE RUMBLE

During the 2019 *Royal Rumble* pay-per-view, Nia Jax made history. Not only did she roll through Superstars in the Women's Royal Rumble Match, but she also attacked R-Truth and snatched his spot in the Men's Royal Rumble—and became the first person to participate in two Royal Rumble matches in the same night. Nia was eliminated by Becky Lynch in the Women's Rumble. In the Men's Rumble, she tossed Mustafa Ali out of the ring. It took a triple attack by Rey Meysterio, Dolph Ziggler, and Randy Orton—including an RKO—to eliminate Nia.

A MATCH WITH NO RULES

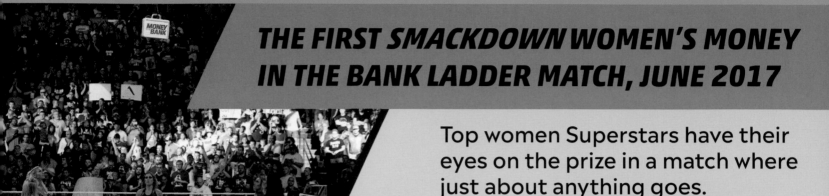

THE FIRST *SMACKDOWN* WOMEN'S MONEY IN THE BANK LADDER MATCH, JUNE 2017

Top women Superstars have their eyes on the prize in a match where just about anything goes.

The Money in the Bank case dangles above the ring as the Superstars prepare for battle.

Carmella is on the receiving end of a powerful kick from Charlotte Flair.

With the words, "Let's do something historic," Shane McMahon announced the first-ever women's Money in the Bank Ladder Match. Charlotte, Becky Lynch, Tamina, Carmella, and Natalya would compete for the contract and a chance to cash it in for the *SmackDown* Women's Championship, held by Naomi.

WHAT GOES UP...

The bell rang as the Superstars eyed the Money in the Bank briefcase dangling 15 feet (4.6 meters) above the ring. Everyone's first instinct was to roll out of the ring to grab a ladder—everyone but Tamina. She used her spot on the mat to block the other Superstars from getting back in. Charlotte finally managed to remove her from her post with a suplex.

Ladders flew. Natalya superplexed Becky directly into a steel rung, then grabbed another ladder and started to climb. She had her hands on the case when Charlotte grabbed her boot. Natalya kicked her down three times

before Charlotte managed to pull her into a devastating Electric Chair Drop. Charlotte tried to set up the ladder again, but Natalya batted her away with another one. Then Natalya wrapped Becky up in her signature Sharpshooter and flipped Charlotte with a butterfly suplex. Becky finally slowed Natalya down by slingshotting her into a pile of ladders. Becky then made a run for the briefcase. Carmella pulled her down, then Charlotte tried her luck, and Tamina pulled her down. Phew!

...MUST COME DOWN

Realizing that she'd better start eliminating her competition, Charlotte climbed to the top rope and took aim at Natalya and Tamina outside of the ring. Hurtling through the air, she landed a spectacular moonsault to knock them both out. While all three were recovering, Carmella began to climb for the briefcase again, but Becky pulled her into a powerbomb.

With all the other Superstars dazed, Becky seized the moment and started climbing toward the case. But just as she reached it, James

Tamina tips Charlotte and Carmella off the ladder, keeping the briefcase safely out of their grasp.

In a questionable victory, Carmella becomes the first Ms. Money in the Bank.

"**You better believe I'm not here for girl power!**"

—CARMELLA

Ellsworth, who had accompanied Carmella to the ring, grabbed the ladder's base and flung Becky from the top. Carmella, still woozy from the powerbomb, couldn't climb, even with a clear path. So James clambered up and dropped the case right into Carmella's hands. The first rule of Ladder Matches is: There are no rules. So Carmella was declared the winner, even though a non-legal man made her the first Ms. Money in the Bank.

Charlotte launches a spectacular moonsault into Natalya and Tamina.

TAKING HOPE GLOBAL

RAW WOMEN'S CHAMPIONSHIP MATCH, ABU DHABI, UAE, DECEMBER 7, 2017

In 2017, *RAW* Superstars took off to Abu Dhabi, in the United Arab Emirates, to battle in a *WWE LIVE* event. In the Zayed Sports City Tennis Stadium, which can hold 37,500 people, Alexa Bliss defended her championship against Sasha Banks in the first WWE women's match ever in the Emirates. In preparation for this historic event, special full-cover body gear was created for the Superstars to respect the Emirates' traditions. Because this was such a momentous match, Alexa and Sasha were nervous beforehand.

But when the Superstars got to the ring, the WWE Universe showed its full support. Fans from all over the Middle East had joined them to take part in the historic event.

Sasha dominated the first half of the match, keeping Alexa reeling from quick jabs and kicks. But Alexa, who battled the ref almost as much as she fought Sasha, turned the tables and tied The Boss up in a tight chokehold. Shaking Alexa loose, Sasha reversed and maneuvered "The Goddess" into a Bank Statement submission hold.

Eventually, Alexa broke free and pinned Sasha to retain her championship. In a match that Sasha said made for "legit goosebumps," the WWE Universe began to chant, "This is hope." Support for WWE's Women's Evolution had spread across the world.

> **"It was almost like a WrestleMania moment."**
>
> —ALEXA BLISS

Sasha Banks nearly forces Alexa Bliss to submit via a painful Bank Statement.

Alexa holds up the Women's Championship title in triumph.

Sasha delivers a painful blow momentarily stunning "The Goddess."

Alexa flips over "The Boss" as she lays on the mat and turns the tides of the match.

113

ASUKA TOPS THE RUMBLE

THE FIRST-EVER WOMEN'S ROYAL RUMBLE MATCH

Almost 20 years to the day after the first WWE *Royal Rumble*, 30 women Superstars would make history...

Sasha Banks and Becky Lynch are first up; Becky soon has Sasha in her Dis-Arm-Her hold.

With the names of all the woman Superstars who couldn't be there on the night written on her right arm, Lita targets Becky and Sasha.

A new day was dawning in the women's division. On January 28, 2018, The Wells Fargo Center in Philadelphia, Pennsylvania, would host the first Women's Royal Rumble Match. To mark this historic occasion, Stephanie McMahon joined the announce team ringside.

Per Royal Rumble Match rules, the competitors who drew the first and second spots would begin the match. Every 90 seconds after the first bell, a new Superstar would enter the ring. If a Superstar went over the top rope and both of their feet touched the ground, they would be eliminated.

Sitting ringside in the front row: *RAW* Women's Champion Alexa Bliss and *SmackDown* Women's Champion Charlotte Flair. The winner of the Royal Rumble Match would win a shot at either woman for the title of her choice at *WrestleMania 34*. As the match began, the fans were on their feet in expectation. They would not be disappointed...

Cleverly avoiding elimination, Naomi tiptoes along the top of the barricade.

Trish Stratus, Natalya, Bayley, the Bella Twins, and Sasha Banks team up to eject the formidable Nia Jax from the competition.

The Bella Twins make sure Bayley is sent out of the action for good.

Down to the final two: 25th entrant Asuka hangs on and uses the power of her legs to drag Nikki Bella over the top rope and onto the apron.

Asuka weighs up which prize to go for at WrestleMania: Charlotte Flair's SmackDown Title or Alexa Bliss's RAW Championship.

FRIENDS BECOME FOES

ELIMINATION CHAMBER 2018

Alexa Bliss defended the *RAW* Women's Championship against Sasha Banks, Mickie James, Mandy Rose, Sonya Deville, Sasha Banks, and Bayley in the first women's Elimination Chamber Match.

The women's division's first Elimination Chamber pitted friends against each other to prove that when push comes to shove, every Superstar will put her alliances to one side and fight for herself. Alexa Bliss had to defend her *RAW* Women's Championship against her friend Mickie James, Absolution members Mandy Rose and Sonya Deville, and friends Bayley and Sasha Banks. Under *Elimination Chamber* rules, two Superstars start in the ring, while the others are locked away in pods. Every five minutes, a pod opens at random and another Superstar joins the fray. Superstars are eliminated by pinfall or submission on the mat.

GETTING BY WITH A LITTLE HELP

Bayley and Sonya Deville started in the ring and traded hits equally. Just as they began to use the chamber itself as a weapon, a pod opened. Mandy Rose was released. Bayley would have to survive the next five minutes alone against the Absolution teammates. The pair started a joint attack on Bayley, but she held on until her friend Sasha was released from the next pod.

Sasha singlehandedly slowed Absolution's momentum. While Sasha worked them both at the turnbuckle, Bayley used the time to get back on her feet and help Sasha with Sonya. Mandy Rose intervened to help her friend, but became Sasha's target for a serious Backstabber move, which went right into a Bank Statement. When Sonya tried to help Mandy, Bayley tackled her. Forced to submit, Mandy Rose tapped out for the first elimination.

Moments later, Mickie James was released. She immediately attacked Banks and then Bayley. When Sonya got back on her feet and whipped Mickie into the cage, Mickie used it to her advantage and flipped Sonya into

Sonya Deville tugs Bayley down from the side of the chamber.

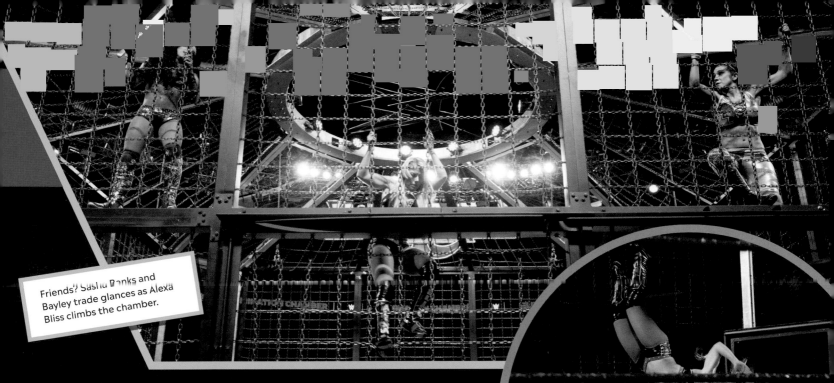

Friends? Sasha Banks and Bayley trade glances as Alexa Bliss climbs the chamber.

Sasha Banks gets her knees up as Alexa aims to land a punishing Twisted Bliss.

a hurricanrana, stopping the assault. With a wild look in her eye, Mickie climbed the chamber to the top of a pod, took aim, and leaped to cover Sonya. By the count of three, Sonya was eliminated. Bayley then intercepted Mickie with a big Bayley-to-Belly Suplex for her elimination.

AND THEN THERE WERE THREE

Friends Bayley and Sasha exchanged a knowing look, then turned toward Alexa Bliss, the final Superstar still in a pod, and waited. As the pod opened, Bayley and Sasha lunged—but Alexa slid the door right back into place and snuck out the back. She began to climb, with Bayley and Sasha in pursuit. Sasha intercepted Alexa on top of a pod. As Bayley reached for a hand up, Sasha gave her a big boot to the face; both Bayley and the WWE Universe were stunned. Alexa used the fractured friendship to her advantage, and, as Bayley went to pin Banks after a big Bayley-to-Belly Suplex, Alexa slid in and rolled Bayley up for the elimination. Ready to end the match, Alexa climbed the ropes and lined up for a Twisted Bliss, but Sasha got her knees up as Alexa landed. Then Sasha flew at Alexa but put

her own leg right through the chamber. Again, Alexa pounced and knocked her with her knee.

Alexa climbed to the top of a pod, hoping the extra height would make for an even more punishing Twisted Bliss. But Sasha was ready and turned the landing into a Bank Statement. Alexa broke free. As Sasha climbed the ropes and headed for the top of a pod, Alexa grabbed her, smashed her into the side of the pod, and pulled her into massive DDT from the top rope. After the three-count, Sasha was eliminated and Alexa retained her title and punched her ticket to *WrestleMania*.

After the match—with the fans chanting "You deserve it!"—a tearful Alexa claimed her victory for "every little girl and woman at home in the audience who have ever dreamed big." She then dried her eyes and, suddenly switching to a more antagonistic mode, said, after looking at everyone in the audience, "the reality is... that none of you will ever accomplish any of your dreams!"

Alexa Bliss retains her championship despite the brutal chamber experience.

RONDA ROUSEY
"THE BADDEST WOMAN ON THE PLANET"

A former medal-winning Olympian, mixed martial artist, and UFC fighter, "Rowdy" Ronda Rousey packs a punch unlike any other Superstar.

How do you become the "Baddest Woman on the Planet?" If you are Ronda Rousey, you start training in judo at age 11, become an Olympian at 17, win a bronze medal at 21, become the first woman in UFC at 25, and have a record-setting run as UFC Women's Bantamweight Champion for three straight years. You would then set sights on the "Grandest Stage of Them All," *WrestleMania*.

Ronda's first WWE match was at *WrestleMania 34*, when she joined another former Olympian, Kurt Angle, in a Mixed Tag Team Match against Triple H and Stephanie McMahon, collectively known as The Authority. Angle and Triple H locked up first. When a roughed-up Angle finally made the tag, Ronda surged into the ring and showed Stephanie just how bad she could be. It was a brutal match, with The Authority doling out as much punishment as they took from the former Olympians. But Ronda and Kurt prevailed. She made Stephanie submit with her trademark Armbar and proved she was ready to battle for the *RAW* Women's Title.

After Alexa Bliss interfered in Ronda's first championship shot against Nia Jax at *Money in the Bank*, *RAW* General Manager Kurt Angle organized a Ronda–Alexa title bout for *SummerSlam 2018*. Ronda dominated Alexa in the match and easily took the title.

The "Rowdy One" reigned for a record 232 days before she faced Becky Lynch and Charlotte Flair in a historic Winner-Takes-All Triple Threat Match at *WrestleMania 35* that ended in a controversial finish. Lynch pinned Ronda, but replays later showed that Ronda's shoulders may have been up before the three-count.

Ronda always insists on competing against the best in the business and needs her competitors to be at the top of their game. The WWE Universe has never seen a competitor like Rousey before, and she's determined to make the women's division the best it can be—one Armbar at a time, if need be.

Ronda launches herself at Becky Lynch and Charlotte Flair at *WrestleMania 35*.

> ## "I want my opponent to be looking me in the eye and primed to fight."
>
> —RONDA ROUSEY

Stephanie McMahon has some harsh words for Ronda Rousey at *WrestleMania 31*.

CHALLENGING AUTHORITY

Even before she signed her contract with the McMahons, "Rowdy" Ronda was tangling with management. At *WrestleMania 31*, as Stephanie McMahon and Triple H took full credit for WWE's success and basked in their power, The Rock arrived to set the record straight. "You don't own them, and you damn sure don't own The Rock," he said. Stephanie McMahon fired back: "Without Rock," he said. Stephanie McMahon fired back: "Without the McMahons, there would be no Rock"—and slapped "The Great One." Announcing that he would never hit a woman, The Rock pulled Ronda Rousey out of the audience and said his very good friend would be happy to. The Rock attacked Triple H and then Ronda bounced Triple H out of the ring. Then she turned on Stephanie and came just short of breaking her arm. "Now that's what's called being owned," The Rock concluded.

> ## "I feel like Ronda is home here."
>
> —STEPHANIE MCMAHON

WHO ARE THE REAL

One name, two factions: some of WWE's toughest female Superstars battle for the chance to be named for one of WWE's most prestigious male teams.

Taking inspiration from the famed sports entertainment stable The Four Horsemen—Ric Flair, Ole and Arn Anderson, and Tully Blanchard—the Four Horsewomen of NXT includes Charlotte, Becky Lynch, Bayley, and Sasha Banks. Sasha claimed the team came up with the name after the friends faced each other in a Fatal 4-Four Way Match at *NXT TakeOver* and flashed four fingers in photos after the match.

The nickname was once attributed to the male Superstars who were making changes in WWE, but this female foursome insist they took the name because of their strong friendship. "There will never be a group like the four of us ever again," Charlotte proclaimed.

The Four Horsewomen of MMA (left to right): Marina Shafir, Jessamyn Duke, Shayna Baszler, and Ronda Rousey.

"This is real, and it's personal... I mean, they don't even like each other... This isn't for show. This is for life for us."

—RONDA ROUSEY

FOUR HORSEWOMEN?

But there is a problem: Ronda Rousey claimed her MMA crew were The Four Horsewomen long before they joined WWE. Consisting of Rousey, Shayna Baszler, Jessamyn Duke, and Marina Shafir, the stable members have been watching each other's backs for years. The Four Horsewomen of MMA were ringside at *WrestleMania 31* when The Rock pulled Ronda into an altercation with Stephanie McMahon and Triple H. The stable was also ringside—and interfering in the ring—to help Shayna Baszler defeat Kairi Sane during *WWE Evolution*.

There's no doubt all the Horsewomen are exceptional athletes, paving the way for women everywhere. The WWE Universe will just have to wait and see which team wins a Horsewomen vs. Horsewomen face-off.

> **"I think the biggest thing that we share is our love for this."**
>
> —SASHA BANKS

The Four Horsewomen of WWE (left to right): Charlotte Flair, Sasha Banks, Becky Lynch, and Bayley.

WWE EVOLUTION

For the first time in WWE history, female Superstars owned the ring in their very own pay-per-view show.

Nia Jax celebrates her 20-Superstar Battle Royal win.

On October 28, 2018, main roster Superstars were joined by WWE legends for an unforgettable night of sports entertainment. Beth Phoenix and Renee Young joined Michael Cole on commentary, and a capacity crowd at the Nassau Coliseum, Long Island, got ready to witness history in the making. Between matches, Superstars reflected on how far the women's division had come. *WWE Evolution*, the first all-female pay-per-view event, was a night that dazzled; a night that shocked; a night of hard work, fun, and respect fully worthy of the women's division.

JUST FOR KICKS

First up was a tag team match made in women's division heaven. Best friends Trish Stratus and Lita faced Mickie James and Alicia Fox. In the same arena where she got her start, Trish took on her old nemesis Mickie as the crowd chanted, "You've still got it." Lita dusted off a big Litacanrana move, and Trish hit a Stratusfaction. Alicia and Mickie tried to run away, but their opponents wouldn't let them leave. Mickie landed a big neckbreaker move on Lita. But Trish and Lita pulled through; Lita launched into a Litasault and Trish hit Mickie with a Chick Kick to finish the match.

A BATTLE FOR THE FUTURE

Next was a ring-shaking 20-Superstar Battle Royal Match. The last Superstar in the ring would have a title opportunity at a Women's Championship Match. To be eliminated, Superstars had to be sent over the top rope, with both feet hitting the ground.

The ring swarmed with Superstars of today and yesterday. The IIconics tag team made the mistake of scoffing at the legends in the ring, so they were the first to go, ousted by Ivory, Alundra Blayze, and

Michelle McCool, among others. Then current Superstars attacked with simultaneous suplexes. This big slam was immediately followed by... a dance break, of all things, with Carmella and Ivory busting moves.

Superstars were tossed out of the ring one by one. One of the few still in the ring, Ember Moon eliminated both Asuka and Tamina, leaving just Nia Jax between her and a future Women's Championship opportunity. Ember was just muscling Nia over the top rope when Zelina Vega appeared and pushed both Superstars over the rope. Thinking she'd won, Zelina began to celebrate. But she'd only succeeded in knocking Nia and Ember to the outside edge. Nia plucked Zelina from the mat and launched her out of the ring. Luckily, Tamina was there to break her fall. Nia then turned her attention to Ember, who fought until Nia bounced her off the mat and out of the ring.

Trish Stratus delivers a devastating move that floors her opponent Mickie James.

A FANTASTIC FINAL

The third match on the card was the 2018 Mae Young Classic tournament final. Australia's Toni Storm and Japan's Io Shirai met in a hard-hitting, high-flying matchup refereed by WWE's first woman ref, Jessika Carr. "Genius of the Sky" Io stunned the WWE Universe and Toni with a gravity-defying moonsault outside the ring. But Toni won the match—and the tournament—by breaking Io's second moonsault with her knees and landing a Storm Zero slam.

TRIPLE TAG TEAM

Fourth up was a triple tag team match: the Riott Squad (Ruby Riott, Liv Morgan, and Sarah Logan) vs. Bayley, Sasha Banks, and Natalya. The Riott Squad moved so well it was as though they shared a brain and body. When Ruby laid out Sasha and aimed to finish the match with a big leap from the top rope, Bayley slid in to save the day. In an impressively timed one-two-three succession, Natalya powerbombed Liv Morgan, Bayley leaped from the top rope and hit Liv with an elbow drop, then Sasha landed a frog splash on Liv. The pin was quick.

UP NXT

The previous year's Mae Young Classic finalists, Kairi Sane and Shayna Baszler, met again, but this time, Kairi was defending her NXT Women's Title. It was a punishing battle, with Kairi landing some huge moves, but ultimately taking a lot of punishment from Shayna. With interference from the Four Horsewomen from MMA, Kairi didn't stand a chance, and the title passed to Shayna.

STILL STANDING

After weeks of increasing tensions, the first-ever Last Woman Standing Match seemed the only way to settle the score between Charlotte Flair and Becky Lynch. No tap outs, no pins—just a bruising battle until one Superstar couldn't make a ten count. The prize: the *SmackDown* Women's Championship, then held by Becky. Katana sticks, steel chairs, and an announce table were just a few of the tools used to inflict damage. In the end, Becky powerbombed Charlotte from the top rope straight through a table, and the ref finally got to ten. Becky retained her title, breaking Charlotte's pay-per-view-winning streak in the process.

Ronda Rousey hoists both Bellas onto her shoulders before slamming them down to the mat.

RONDA UNDER SIEGE

In the main event, Ronda Rousey defended her *RAW* Women's Championship against Nikki Bella (and Brie Bella, too). Nikki didn't think Ronda had enough respect for the Divas Era and didn't deserve to be champion. Ronda tossed Nikki around the ring, but Nikki got the upper hand by distracting the ref so Brie could slam Ronda into the LED ringpost. While Ronda was stunned, Nikki went to work. She squeezed Ronda into a chokeslam and nailed her with a Rack Attack 2.0. Ronda dug deep and hoisted both Bellas onto her shoulders for a big drop. Then she slammed Brie into an announce table to prevent any more interference. When Ronda intercepted Nikki on the top rope and pulled her down into an armbar, Nikki quickly tapped out and Ronda retained her championship.

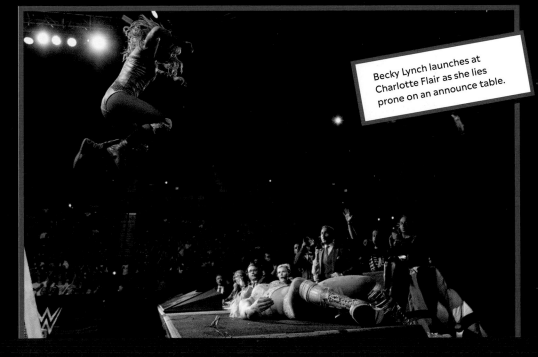

Becky Lynch launches at Charlotte Flair as she lies prone on an announce table.

WINNER TAKES ALL

WRESTLEMANIA 35: BECKY LYNCH VS. CHARLOTTE FLAIR VS. RONDA ROUSEY

Both *RAW* and *SmackDown* women's titles were at stake as *WrestleMania 35*'s main event became a Triple Threat Match.

Charlotte dangles Ronda over the ropes as Becky slides in with a kick.

Charlotte shows her strength by pulling Becky into a Spanish Fly maneuver.

Ronda racks Becky over her shoulders and prepares to spin her into a drop.

The lead-up to this historic, first-ever women's main event match at *WrestleMania* was turbulent. Charlotte Flair, handpicked by Vince McMahon, was set to challenge Ronda Rousey for the *RAW* Women's Championship. And Becky Lynch, who had originally been set to face Rousey, had spent the weeks beforehand with a warrant out for her arrest for attacking Ronda.

Ronda, refusing to face "chosen challengers," persuaded Stephanie McMahon to let Becky take part in the *WrestleMania* main event. With Charlotte having won the *SmackDown* Championship, the upcoming match had become a Triple Threat Winner Takes All main event!

THREE'S A CROWD

In a Triple Threat Match, Superstars not only have to pin to win, they have to prevent anyone else from pinning. The bell rang, and the action quickly moved outside the ring. Becky slammed Ronda into the LED ringpost, then Charlotte sent Ronda through a barricade. With Ronda dazed, Becky and Charlotte returned to the mat for some one-on-one time. But Ronda didn't stay down for long. Charlotte flipped her over the top rope and dangled her above the floor, then Becky charged and kicked

Ronda, who dropped to the floor.

With Becky and Charlotte back fighting each other, Charlotte tried a big moonsault. But Becky caught her and wrenched Charlotte into a Dis-arm-her. Back on her feet and smack-talking again, Ronda weathered Flair Chops until Charlotte twisted her upside down. Before Ronda could submit, Becky slammed both of them to the mat. Becky tried to pin Ronda, but was unsuccessful. Becky then covered Charlotte, but she also kicked out.

The match seemed to be Becky's when she turned a clash with Charlotte on the top rope into a huge Bexsploder, but Charlotte still kicked out. As they recuperated, Ronda leaped in for a double crossbody cover, but no dice. Frustrated, Ronda tried to wrap them into a double Arm Bar, but the two muscled her up and repeatedly slammed her to the mat. No one was going to give in. The Superstars then went into annihilation mode. Becky tried to twist Ronda into a Dis-arm-her hold. Charlotte spun Becky off the top

rope in a crazy Spanish fly and wrapped Ronda's legs around the LED ringpost *and* into a figure four leglock. Exasperated, Becky pulled a table out from under the ring and she and Ronda put Charlotte through it.

With Charlotte out of commission, Becky and Ronda sneered at each other. Ronda flipped Becky into a Piper's Pit maneuver, but Becky pinned Ronda's shoulders and got the count. Ronda's first loss by pinfall lead to another first: Becky became the first women's double title-holder.

> **"Everything about this... feels like it was so meant to be."**
>
> —BECKY LYNCH

Becky collides with Charlotte's high kick over the ropes.

Becky interrupts Charlotte's submission hold on Ronda by slamming both Superstars.

Becky Lynch survives the triple threat, becoming Becky Two Belts in the process.

INDEX

Project Editor Pamela Afram
Senior Editor Alastair Dougall
Senior Designer Nathan Martin
Editor Julia March
Editorial Assistant Vicky Armstrong
Designers Thelma-Jane Robb, Gary Hyde
Senior Pre-Production Producer Marc Staples
Senior Producer Mary Slater
Managing Editor Sarah Harland
Managing Art Editor Vicky Short
Art Director Lisa Lanzarini
Publisher Julie Ferris

Global Publishing Manager Steve Pantaleo
Vice President, Interactive Products Ed Kiang
Vice President, Consumer Products Sylvia Lee
Senior Vice President, Consumer Products Sarah Cummins
Vice President—Photography Bradley Smith
Photo department Josh Tottenham, Frank Vitucci,
Georgiana Dallas, Jamie Nelson, Melissa Halladay
**Senior Vice President, Assistant General Counsel—
Intellectual Property** Lauren Dienes-Middlen
Senior Vice President, Creative Services Stan Stanski
Creative Director John Jones
Project Manager Brent Mitchell

First published in Great Britain in 2020
by Dorling Kindersley Limited.
80 Strand, London, WC2R 0RL
A Penguin Random House Company

Page design copyright © 2020 Dorling Kindersley Limited
A Penguin Random House Company

10 9 8 7 6 5 4 3 2 1
001–316380–May/2020

A CIP catalogue record for this book is available
from the British Library.

978-0-24140-927-5

Photographs on pages 6 (Mildred Burke), 7 (Judy Grable),
and 88 (Peter Maivia) by *Pro Wrestling Illustrated*.

Printed and bound in China

A WORLD OF IDEAS:
SEE ALL THERE IS TO KNOW

www.dk.com
www.wwe.com